Two week loan

Please return on or before the last date stamped below.
Charges are made for late return.

18 OCT 1995
CANCELLED

17 MAR 2000

26 FEB 1996
CANCELLED

CANCELLED

15 OCT 1997
CANCELLED

2 CANCELLED

WITHDRAWN

CANCELLED 1997

2 3 OCT 1998
CANCELLED

- 8 DEC 1999

CANCELLED

Action Research and Organizational Change

Peter A. Clark

Action Research and Organizational Change

Harper & Row, Publishers
London New York Evanston San Francisco

Published by Harper & Row Ltd
28 Tavistock Street, London WC2E 7 PN

Standard Book Number 06–318001–4 (cloth)
Standard Book Number 06–318004–9 (paper)

Printed by Unwin Brothers Limited
The Gresham Press, Old Woking, Surrey, England
A member of the Staples Printing Group

Contents

Acknowledgements

Action Research and Organizational Change is based on field and literature searches that I conducted in collaboration with colleagues on sponsored research and the Social Science Research Council program of investigators from the Centre for the Utilization of Social Science Research, Loughborough University of Technology.

This book reports part of the programme of comparative researches on factors influencing the utilization of the social sciences. My role has been that of researcher, and subsequently co-investigator. The over-all direction and leadership is provided by Professor Albert Cherns, without whose optimism and anlytical resourcefulness the programme would not have been possible. From the Centre for Utilization of Social Science Research my six colleagues on the SSRC program have been a source of stimulation and encouragement. Additionally Professor Jim Taylor, formerly at Michigan University and now at the Centre for Organizational Research, University of California, Los Angeles, gave generously with suggestions for analysis joining the first periods of thinking and writing. In the field, Bernard Leach (now at Manchester Business School), Chris Eling (now at Philips Industries), Pauline Mistry, Wynne Harries and Doug Spencer, Ken Levine, Tim Sparrow, and Stephen Parrot made important contributions.

My experience of applied and action research was largely due to the imaginative thinking of Jack Wessel and David Boewn between 1960 and 1963; later to Tony Davies, Andrew Reid, and Leslie Hallam.

I was fortunate in being able to draw on the resources and advice of the following during the construction and development of the manuscript: Professor Richard Walton (Harvard Business School), Professor H. A. Thompson (McGill), Professor Mark van de Vall (Buffalo), Dr Keith Thurley (LSE), Mr Richard Brown (Durham University), Miss Lisl Klein (Tavistock IHR).

My researches on the practitioner-sponsor relationship was greatly assisted by discussions with Professor Herman Hutte, Groningen University. Dutch social scientists have been extraordinarily effective

ix

in applied and action research and my analysis of the organizational context of these activities benefited from discussions with Dr Reinaud, Dr Maarten van Gils; Dr Cees Luscuere; Peter van Dun; and many others.

I am grateful to Professor Lou G. Davies (UCLA), Professor Phil Herbert, and Dr Einar Throsrud (Work Research Institutes, Oslo) for extending my understanding about socio-technical analysis and its interface with other approaches to organizational change.

Dr John Child, Senior Research Officer at the London Graduate Business School, encouraged me to write, ensured the smooth co-operation with my publisher, freely exchanged ideas and suggestions, and read drafts of the script.

The London office of Harper & Row organized the administrative aspect with great care and efficiency. Mrs Gloria Brentnall was all good secretaries should be, the flexible resource typing sections and checking the manuscript. Mrs Jenny Wilcox undertook the brunt of the typing.

Permission from Dr Gunnar Hjeholt to use and refer to his work 'Training for Reality' is gratefully acknowledged. I also wish to thank John Wiley & Sons, Inc. for pernission to print Figure 2 and the Institute for Social Research, University of Michigan for permission to print Figures 3, 4 and 5.

Finally, I must thank my family for tolerating yet another withdrawal to the isolation of a Norfolk coastal village during the first phase of writing and then later into the Welsh valleys. By the time of the completion of the manuscript my son Giles had decided to call me Peter rather than Daddy, and Gemma was too young to appreciate the subtle change. My wife, Jennifer, organized family life round the periods of writing and reflection and was a major contributor in making the book a reality.

It is customary to stress that those one meets and works with are only responsible for the good points and the author for the weaknesses. This seems to me to be an untenable position. Whilst it is true that the author decides the formula, it is also true that I have been influenced by those I have worked with. I trust my interpretation does justice to their thinking.

Foreword

When we set up in 1967 the Centre for Utilization of Social Science at Loughborough, with the help of a grant from the British Social Science Research Council, we were embarking on uncharted waters. Peter Clark, who had recently been appointed as Lecturer in Sociology at the University and who had previous experience in management services in industry and of teaching and research in a management institute, joined the Centre and quickly became the director of our first action research project, which he has now published in the form of an intensive case analysis in 'Organisational Design: Theory and Practice'. As co-director of the Centre, he has during the past five years led teams engaged in action research projects which were undertaken with the dual aims of utilizing knowledge and studying the processes involved in getting knowledge into action. He has also directed the only graduate programme in social science utilization so far established, a microcosm of the Graduate School of Applied Behavioral Science recommended in the BASS Report* but nowhere implemented.

These five years have been busy and eventful. As a result of our experiences in a number of industries, in military establishments and in the hospitals service, we now know a good deal more about the problems and advantages of carrying out action research. And because our aim was to study action research itself, Peter Clark has been concerned all along to locate what we have been doing and what we have learned on the map of knowledge, constructing the chart we lacked to begin with. He has thus been able to produce a comparative analysis of action research and its theoretical basis. We have come to regard action research not only as a technique for engaging with organizations but also as a methodology for obtaining otherwise unavailable information and, above all, as a strategy for the diffusion of knowledge. This

* 'The Behavioral and Social Sciences: Outlooks and Needs', National Academy of Sciences, Washington D.C., 1969.

book represents, therefore, not only an addition to our knowledge about action research, but a systematization of the field and a substantial breaking of new ground.

ALBERT B. CHERNS

CHAPTER 1

Introduction

In every field of human activity, more and more people are concerned with using the behavioural sciences to facilitate planned changes. Examples of such work are plentiful in industry, education, the military, in hospitals, prisons, the retail trades, and in government. But the student and researcher reading accounts of the application of behavioural science in all these areas is faced by three major difficulties. First, there appear to be very few successful innovations, yet the literature is replete with case studies of success stories. Second, the predominant explanation of why innovations fail assumes the existence of an initial resistance to change, yet there are many examples of failures in instances where the initial resistance was low or almost non-existent. Third, there are many individual case studies, a number of useful collections of readings representing particular schools of thought, and a few examples of systematic research, but there is no single text that relates the case studies, the readings, and the theories. Consequently, considerable confusion exists about organizational change and the uses to which behavioural science can be put in achieving change.

Within this context, there has been an increase in the demand for action research as a strategy for facilitating and learning about organizational change. To speak of action research implies that other kinds of research are dissimilar. Is there one variety of research or several? If there are several, how is action research distinctive and in what ways can it facilitate organizational change? How do we establish criteria for recognizing situations in which each kind of research is relevant and by which performance can be judged? These questions are discussed in Chapter 2, illustrated in the case studies presented in Chapter 4, and analysed further in subsequent chapters.

Planned organizational change is typically considered by behavioural scientists to mean using various forms of group experience, structured and unstructured, as a way of making people more open to change. This approach assumes that people's initial resistance to change is of critical importance. Yet in a research study on the attempt by sympathetic school teachers to implement a new teaching method known as the catalytic role model, Gross, Giacquinta, and Bernstein (1971) have clearly shown that the teachers were highly sympathetic but that the innovation failed. This study is one example of many which suggest that the context of the organization into which an innovation is being introduced requires careful mapping to reveal its actual structural and attitudinal profile so that the method of implementing the innovation can be matched to the situation.

In practice and in theory it is sensible to view any organization as a configuration of interacting variables, some of which are highly interdependent. Thus, in choosing points for intervention to achieve planned change, one begins to find several possible points and to discover that change may be facilitated by manipulating several variables, some of which may affect change indirectly. The case studies (Chapter 4) illustrate these observations. They also reveal the existence of the issue of problem ownership. Curiously, professionals tend to think of problem ownership as a peculiarity of the thinking of employees in craft occupations, like ship builders in the United Kingdom or longshoremen in North America. But problem ownership is also the dynamic of relations within and between disciplines in the universities; between the universities and the professions; and within the professions operating inside the organizations that use behavioural science. Innovations may fail because the behavioural scientists facilitating the innovation may not be aware of how existing patterns of ownership influence outcomes.

In cases where problem ownership by behavioural scientists becomes established and routinized, we find that particular solutions for widely experienced problems tend to become well known and formalized. The catalytic role model (Gross et al., 1971, pp. 11–15) is novel and poorly articulated; in contrast, the Managerial Grid is well established and relatively formalized.

Approaches to organizational change vary in their selected points of intervention, in the characteristics of problem ownership, and with respect to the degree of formalization. Considerable controversies surround these topics, and Chapter 3 is designed to introduce the main ideas in a way that makes the basis of the controversies clear.

Chapter 4 contains seven case studies selected from various contexts and illustrating different approaches to organizational change. These studies present a good picture of the diversity of approaches that are available, but they do not resolve the issues so far raised; these are tackled in the subsequent chapters.

An initial distinction of some importance is that between sponsors of behavioural science and the practitioners who advise and undertake parts of the diagnosis and change programme. Chapter 5 describes the main roles within the sponsoring system and main roles of the practitioners, suggesting that the relationship between them is best understood as an uneasy partnership. Considerable emphasis is given to showing both the complexity of roles and also the organizational context. This latter aspect is further developed in Chapter 9, Section 1.

It has been said that behavioural science practitioners apply valid knowledge through a collaborative relationship, but what do these terms mean? And does the relationship between practitioners and sponsors *have* to be collaborative?

Chapter 6 defines valid knowledge, identifying its essential characteristics, contrasting the practitioner and the scientist with respect to their definitions of knowledge, and emphasizing the role of theory when using behavioural science. This chapter demonstrates that within the broad spectrum of available knowledge for use, and points of intervention for applying knowledge, there are various specialisms already evident which reflect specific areas of focus for practitioners. For example, exponents of approaches known as organizational development tend to focus upon people's attitudes, aiming to transform these, whilst other approaches focus upon structural variables, regarding attitudes as less important or as open to indirect change.

Chapter 7 examines the most popular model for the relationship between practitioners and sponsors, that is, the collaborative model. Several versions of this are examined and compared with other competing models identified in the case studies. The analysis at this stage begins to connect the focus of the practitioner with the kinds of role model preferred by asking the question, are some role models more appropriate to particular kinds of focus? For example, should the practitioner be an expert rather than a collaborator if the focus is upon structural, task, or technical variables? Before answering the question we move to a closer examination of intervention strategies in Chapter 8 and discover that the preferred role model is intimately connected with whether the practitioner aims to be directive or non-directive in his relationships with the sponsor. This point leads into an important consideration, namely that organizational change strategies which are systemic in approach contain two important varieties and not just one, as has commonly been assumed. *We distinguish between systemic approaches that are directed at intragroup and intergroup problem solving from those which are more concerned with articulating the relationship between organization and its environment.* The former assumes that the content of ideas in problem solving is adequate but that the relationships between the problem solvers can be improved, while the latter emphasizes that the content of ideas may be inadequate. By adopting this distinction, it is possible to clarify some of issues surrounding the generality of approaches to change based upon group methods and to point to the requirement for alternative strategies when conceptual inputs are important. Chapter 8 also deals with the important issue of whether there are phases or cycles in action research.

The discussion of valid knowledge, role models, and intervention strategies in Chapters 6, 7 and 8 clarifies and reorganizes existing cases and theory but does not directly deal with the context within which action research occurs.

In Chapters 9 and 10, we concentrate on context. Chapter 9 develops the earlier theme of the influence of structural and cultural features on organizational change by giving careful examination to the concept of organization and illustrating the points in two further case studies. One study examines the failure of a plant-wide incentive scheme and the other compares the use of similar roles and intervention strategies in two contrasting organizational contexts.

Chapter 10 develops the themes introduced in the previous chapter by adding an analysis of the sponsor's expectations and situation with respect to the practitioner's role and intervention strategy. It is argued that the controversies regarding particular roles and strategies should be resolved by taking into consideration the sponsor's situation and resources at the start of an organizational change programme. In this way three earlier elements in the analysis are integrated: the focus of the practitioner, the organizational context and sponsor's state, and the selection of the role and intervention strategy.

Privileged access is an implicit characteristic of action research. That is to say, action research as an approach provides the practitioner and scientists with a unique opportunity to observe and examine organizational change as a process. This particular facet requires some brief emphasis, which is given in Chapter 11.

Underlying the examination of organizational change and also that of action research are three main models about the ways in which behavioural science is brought into use. The three main models, introduced and discussed in Chapter 12, have a number of complementary strengths which can be isolated and integrated into a comprehensive perspective.

Chapter 13 identifies the requirements for further research on action research and makes some specific suggestions for postgraduate and undergraduate dissertations.

Finally, Chapter 14 summarises the main points and draws together the arguments previously introduced.

The ordering of the book has been designed to provide a basic introduction to key issues in Chapters 2 and 3, then to present case studies in Chapter 4 so that the reader can test his or her understanding. The cases also provide a good deal of the illustrative material that is used in the analysis throughout the book. These introductory chapters are followed by seven chapters examining key themes and issues. The penultimate chapter deals with the requirements for further research and the final chapter summarizes the analysis. Many examples are drawn from published sources and from my own researches and action research on organizational change.

B

CHAPTER 2

Research: one kind or many?

A leading American psychologist, Sanford (1970), recently revised a statement which he had made some fifteen years previously about the extent of action research in North America. He had been optimistic about the future of action research and considered that it had already become established as a 'research-cum-change' strategy during the early 1950s, but now he feels that action research is not in the mainstream of the social sciences: more specifically, that it never really got off the ground and was condemned to a sort of orphan's role in the social sciences shortly after World War II. Sanford suggests that the earlier optimism was influenced by the great men in action research who were still active. When they retired, it became apparent that there had actually been a sharp separation of research and practice which has had some serious negative consequences for social science. This revised picture of the current state of action research is supported by observations by the experienced British researcher, E. L. Trist (1968), who made similar comments to the 1968 conference in Amsterdam on Applied Psychology, suggesting that the situation in Europe is very similar.

The question arises, Why has action research made so little progress during the past twenty-five years and why are there so few instances of this type of activity? The question is of considerable relevance to our analysis, especially given that there is now increasing interest in North America, Europe, Australasia, and Japan from both policy-makers and researchers. We may note some broad points in our attempt to answer this question. Without doubt, the past twenty-five years have witnessed a sharp increase in public interest in the social and behavioural sciences. An increasing amount of public money has been available for both teaching and research. In this period of expansion, the first post-war leaders in the research field have frequently risen to key positions as deans of faculties, advisers to governments and enterprises, and heads of research agencies. The rate of growth has implied a certain strain on existing resources. The small number of highly skilled professionals

6

once available have been stretched over an ever increasing range of research projects with the consequence that the transmission of certain kinds of research competence became almost impossible. This was not a serious problem for the highly formalized survey instrument, but it was a serious problem with respect to establishing any research activity which required manpower already possessing or having access to the range of analytical skills of the kind evident in, for example, the study of the International Typographical Workers by Lipset, Trow and Coleman.*

During this period of increased financial support for research there was a tendency for research leaders to go for the kinds of project which relied on using the potential provided by improved analysis of data by computer technology. This provided projects that were relatively easy to operate and apparently satisfied the public sponsors. Unfortunately, those methods of research based upon multiple research techniques, such as the comparative case study, were slighted as unscientific, and those establishments which advocated, for example, the case-study investigation as a form of training were regarded as 'soft'. Consequently, since 1945, one particular form of relationship between the social scientist and the layman became popular. This was evaluation research, where the role of the social scientist was to accept the terms of reference and objectives specified by sponsors as desirable and utilize the survey approach to measure the actual situation. The results of this research were then compared with the desired states, usually to reveal a sharp discrepancy.

The post-war period for the social sciences was one in which great stress was given to professionalism and to technical matters of competence in data collection in relation to hypothesis testing. Gouldner (1971), in a striking and entertaining assessment of this approach, argues that the social scientists who undertook research for the state departments and major bureaucracies produced theoryless theories, devoid of substantive concepts and assumptions expressing human behaviour and social relationships. The emphasis was given to apparently neutral research methods and research technologies. Gouldner terms this approach methodological empiricism and argues that its exponents offer sponsors the mantle of measurement and provide scientific sanctioning to policies that emphasize political consensus and

* S. M. Lipset, M. Trow and J. Coleman, 1956, *Union Democracy*, New York: Anchor Books.

hence the methodological empiricists are increasingly becoming the market researchers of the Welfare State.

Unfortunately, the growth of professionalism did not include the kinds of skill required by exponents of action research and more complex approaches to basic researches (see Glaser and Strauss, 1968; Denzin, 1970, chap. 12). Consequently, the research styles of the leading practitioners of these approaches remained both difficult to de-code and largely unavailable to the growing number of graduate social scientists.

Today the situation in which the social sciences engage with sponsors has changed. Increasingly sponsors are sophisticated at employing the data-collecting competences of social scientists and are growing more concerned to learn how such data can be used as a basis for action. Simultaneously with this development, there has come about an imbalance between the supply of social scientists wanting to undertake the kinds of activity we have identified as evaluation research and methodological empiricism and the demand for their services by sponsors. Finally, the social scientist is increasingly faced with the requirement to have privileged access to special situations in order to develop theory and practice, yet the original novelty of being researched has worn thin, and the scientist has to be able to offer something more in order to gain access.

This new situation presents just the kind of challenge that action research can meet. However, action research can only be successful if we have some clear blueprint of what it is, what the main activities look like, how it differs from other kinds of research, and what criterion should be applied to assess its performance. As a first stage in tackling these questions, we examine a five-fold typology of research. My argument is that there are many kinds of research, not just one.

2.1 Typology

In the opening remarks of this chapter the analysis has pointed to the existence of several distinct kinds of research activity with one model predominating, that of methodological empiricism. A major consequence of the existence of the one dominant model is the idea conveyed, frequently unwittingly, that this is both the best and the only model. The question whether it is best can be resolved by examining the appropriateness of any type of research in relation to its stated objectives.

Thus the next task is to establish the means for distinguishing and comparing the varying kinds of research activity that exist. To achieve this we need a typology based on the critical dimensions.* When we have the typology then the process of critical appraisal can begin.

What dimensions should be selected? Of the many possible dimensions, three are frequently referred to, either explicitly or implicitly:

1. Is the research oriented towards the clarification and resolution of a theoretical question arising in the discipline, or is it oriented to the solution of a practical problem in one enterprise?
2. What should be the dominant channel for diffusing the results of the research? This may range from learned journals in the case of theoretically oriented research, to reports to the sponsors within a single enterprise in the case of the solution of a practical problem;
3. What is the direction of the involvement of the researcher with his audience? This may be single or multiple. The single case occurs when the researcher has only one relevant audience – it can be members of the scientific community or sponsors of practical problem research. Multiple directions occur when the researcher is both solving a practical problem and also contributing to the understanding and stock of knowledge of the scientific community.

These three dimensions may be combined to produce a taxonomy of types of research. From the various combinations available, five have been identified, as set out in Table 2.1:

1. Pure basic
2. Basic objective
3. Evaluation
4. Applied
5. Action

The typology has the general advantage of highlighting certain strategic differences between research that is oriented to the development of theory and research designed to solve practical problems, yet it does not exaggerate these differences. It emphasizes the importance of audiences and the chosen channels of diffusion. For example, we would deduce from the theory underlying the typology that very little pure basic research becomes known to the executives in enterprises because

* The typology presented here is developed from that suggested by A. B. Cherns, 1968, pp. 209–218.

TABLE 2.1 *Five types of research*

Research type	Researcher's problem orientation	Dominant diffusion channel	Single or mixed audiences
1. PURE BASIC	Theoretical problem arising in basic discipline	Learned journals	Scientists (single)
2. BASIC OBJECTIVE	General practical problem arising in many contexts	Learned and professional journals	Scientists (and practitioners*)
3. EVALUATION	Practical problem (e.g. success of training schemes)	Mainly sponsoring enterprise	Sponsor (and practitioners) (mixed)
4. APPLIED	Practical problem (e.g. job enrichment)	Only sponsoring enterprise	Sponsor (single)
5. ACTION	Practical problem with theoretical relevance	(1) Reports to sponsor (2) Learned and professional journals	Sponsors Scientists Practitioners (mixed)

* 'Practitioners' refers to graduates of the social sciences working within enter-prises as organizational scientists as distinct from scientists in universities.

they do not typically read the *American Sociological Review, Psychological Bulletin,* or the *European Journal of Sociology.* Similarly, scientists would not, without special efforts, be aware of the content and aims of the many reports given to sponsors in cases where both sponsors and the researcher are only concerned with solving a practical problem. The typology and its underpinning theory explains why the enormous investment in the basic research programmes on organizations has not had, and is unlikely to have, much penetration in the professional community and with sponsors. Thus we have the paradoxical position that large-scale research programmes are justified to the research foundations (as distinct from user-enterprises) by their practical pay offs yet are outside the arena of knowledge for the executive. Indeed, it is doubtful if the socio-organizational perspective exemplified in the work of the contingency theorists (see Section 2.3) has penetrated much beyond the business schools and similar teaching centres.

The typology has the important advantage of disaggregating several kinds of research activity, each with a distinctive configuration of attributes. It is quite clear from the typology that the dominant model of methodological empiricism is not the only form possible or, for that matter, desirable. Most importantly, we can detect that the unique characteristic of action research includes its orientation to the problems of three main audiences: scientists, behavioural science practitioners, sponsors. The next task is to examine each of these five main types in more detail as a basis for outlining the criteria of adequacy for each type.

2.2 Pure basic research

This type of research arises out of the perceived requirements for the development of a basic discipline and is typically oriented towards resolving, or illumination, or exemplifying, a theoretical question. A good example of pure basic research undertaken in the organizational field is that by A. L. Stinchcombe (1959) designed to examine Weber's model of bureaucracy. Stinchcombe argues that bureaucracy as a concept is somewhat nebulous and, further, that single case studies are unlikely to sort out the inherent from the ephemeral connections amongst organizational characteristics. Thus a research design is constructed to contrast the situations of mass production with those of craft production as represented in building construction.

The major differences between the two forms of production are set out in Table 2.2. Stinchcombe argues that the craft skill characteristic of the labour force in the construction industry is efficient because it represents an appropriate form of administration when the enterprise is intimately dependent upon variations in local markets, especially the seasonal variations in the volume and mix of work. This, coupled with the small market for construction firms and the project nature of construction in which the form of organizing is always changing in accordance with the phase of the building, indicates the inappropriateness of bureaucratic administration and the necessity for craft groups. Stinchcombe argues that the professional-craft form of administration and the bureaucratic form are real alternatives. In this way a distinction

TABLE 2.2 *Rational administration: some distinctions*

Feature	Type	
	Craft	Mass Production
1. CRITERION	Products and work process governed by craft principles operated by men doing the work Empirical lore and self-discipline	Product and work process planned in advance by persons not doing the actual work
2. PLANNING	Diffused/general specifications	Centralized with specialists. Detailed specifications. Checking by clerks recording required and actual figures
3. COMMUNICATION e.g. % administration devoted to filing	Complex 20%	Simplified 45–60%
4. Status of key initiators of action programmes	70% are owner/proprietors	60% are professionals
5. Judgement in job	Criteria decentralized to 'face' worker	Criteria centralized; quality control

Based on A. L. Stinchcombe, 1959.

is made between rational administration and bureaucracy, and the latter is defined as a special case of the former.

Stinchcombe uses the differences between construction and mass production to reformulate Weber's ideal type of bureaucracy. His analysis shows that in bureaucracy the following are closely interrelated: continuity of work and status within the administrative system, resolving of decisions at each higher level in the hierarchy, and the existence of files. These three elements are found in mass production but not in construction. In contrast, both types contain: separation of positions in the household from the organization, the allocation of work to those who are competent, payment only in money and regulated by the status of the worker. Stinchcombe develops his analysis further to argue that both bureaucracy (mass production) and professional-craft organization are rational forms of administration with three elements in common. In this way, he develops a line of thinking originally advanced by Weber to resolve a theoretical question arising in the discipline of sociology.

This particular example is of special interest to our analysis because Stinchcombe's work does have a practical implication. He is implicitly outlining a set of functionally connected attributes which may be said to have practical relevance to those designing the organizational systems of enterprises. However, we would expect that this kind of finding would have low diffusion. The expectation may be easily checked. First, Woodward, in researches which were intentionally of a practical nature, being designed to identify solutions to widely experienced practical problems, makes no reference to his work, yet it is intimately relevant to the research undertaken.* Again, Trist *et al.*, in their account of the two forms of work-group organization adopted with the introduction of long-wall coal mining in England, make no explicit cross reference, yet Stinchcombe's findings are of direct relevance and Trist's suggested solution would be theoretically supported by his analysis. We should therefore expect that work undertaken by scientists will not readily find its way into the thinking of those concerned with other kinds of research, irrespective of the relevance of the findings. Typically, pure basic research is at a high level of generality and the primary channel of diffusion is the learned journal. Hence, the feedback of results is not typically to the wider public or to potential users in organizations, but to the 'stock of knowledge' of the scientific community. Consequently, the findings from such work may take some time before they penetrate the practice of professionals within enterprises or become part of the general stock of knowledge. The kinds of knowledge which are perhaps more influential arise from the next type of research.

2.3 Basic objective research

This category of research is concerned with the tackling of a general problem which occurs in some field of the application of knowledge,

* Stinchcombe is not listed in the author index of either *Industrial Organization; Theory and Practice*, 1965, or *Industrial Organization; Behaviour and Control*, 1970.

but it does not aim to provide a prescription for a particular practical problem. Well-known examples in the field of organizational research would include the critical analysis of classical precepts about administration arising from the researches of the late Joan Woodward in Great Britain, and the systematic examination by Lawrence and Lorsch from Harvard of problems of diagnosing the mechanics needed to match the state of differentiation of an enterprise to the requirements of co-ordination and integration. These researches were designed to deal with the general problem of matching the administrative structure of the enterprise to the specific demands, both external and internal, of the tasks which the enterprise was undertaking. The aim was to develop a theory which could be applied across all kinds of organizations: hospitals, the military, industry of all kinds, retail, education.

What are the channels of diffusion for this category of research? The level of generality is high and the primary channels of dissemination are professional journals; the major line of feedback is to the professional community and associated academics. In practice, very little of the perspective of the contingency theorists has penetrated deeply into management education, and even less into, for example, organizational design. There are, however, signs in the United Kingdom arising from initiatives taken by one of the crucially placed Industrial Training Boards that this situation is changing. Generally speaking, basic objective research is publicly funded (e.g. studies of leadership) and increasingly tends to be located in both professional journals and also in the journals of particular occupational groups (e.g. nurses, electrical engineers, chemists). In the case of the early research by Woodward, the Social Science Research Council (U K) encouraged the creation of a cogent, highly readable account in booklet form which became incorporated into the course curricula of, for example, administrators.

2.4　Evaluation research

The aim of evaluation research is to provide an assessment of some aspect of the performance of an enterprise. Typically, evaluation research has included the assessment of the effectiveness of change programmes both within enterprises and, in the recent period, for the assessment of community-based change programmes designed to tackle the issues of poverty, ethnic discrimination, and educational opportunity. The aim of evaluating such programmes is controversial, but

before we examine this issue, we shall set out the main characteristics
of evaluation research.

Evaluation research is aimed at tackling an existing and continuing
practical problem within an enterprise, but it does not include a change
strategy. It is distinguished by its methods and strategy which are at a
high level of generality. The normal programme proceeds as follows:

- – examining the objectives of the enterprise or the selected sub-part
- – identifying the goals of the unit selected
- – establishing specific criteria against which success can be measured
  and devising specific measures
- – carrying out a research study on the selected unit to measure
  performance
- – comparing the actual performance against the goals previously
  established
- – reporting the discrepancy between the desired and the actual
  performance

Evaluation research is frequently and widely used and the results of
such researches are typically only of specific interest to the sponsors and
other implicated parties. The channel of diffusion of these highly
particularistic reports is to the sponsor. Occasionally they may be
published in professional journals because they illustrate a development
in research technology, and additionally, there may be some discussion
of the reports at the local level amongst interested evaluation researchers
in their district branches of professional associations.

Evaluation research is the dominant type of research in the relationships of exchange between social scientists and professional practitioners, and is also, as we noted from the comments of Gouldner, one
which has recently been subjected to considerable criticism. I agree with
many of the expressed doubts about the utility of evaluation research,
especially with respect to the evaluation of change programmes. Before
considering these criticisms, it is relevant to restate our earlier observation that evaluation research was the first major form of exchange
between the scientific community and sponsors in enterprises. The
accommodation largely took the form of the sponsor purchasing two
attributes from the scientist: a sophisticated method of information
collection and the appearance of scientific neutrality – 'it's scientific, it
must be correct'. I have argued against this conception, suggesting that
the distinctive competence of the social scientist is the possession of a

perspective and related set of propositions which embody substantive concepts about human behaviour. The problem of the scientific image of evaluation research and its neglect of social processes within groups and enterprises can be explored in a number of ways. I have selected the controversy surrounding the utility of evaluations of planned change programmes.

It is helpful at this point to follow a distinction between evaluation research which is designed to measure the difference between the states of an enterprise before and after the introduction of a planned change programme – known as summative evaluation – from evaluation research designed to facilitate improvements in planned change strategies – known as formative evaluation (see Scriven, 1967). It is summative evaluation which has been most controversial because the typical situation is one in which an independent team of evaluators is directed to report on success without explaining why a programme was more or less successful. The inability of summative evaluation to reveal the crucial processes underlying success or failure is a sore point with the practitioners who are responsible for introducing the change programmes; there is a well documented line of tension between these two groups which can readily be apprehended by comparing the following two typifications of evaluation research and applied and/or action research as set out in Table 2.3. Given the differences that this Table presents, it is not hard to imagine why exponents of action research programmes feel as they do. In the case of action research programmes, it is not possible to neatly identify the mission – indeed, it might be politically disastrous for the project if this happened. We know from investigation by G. N. Jones of 200 case studies that action programmes are rarely characterized by a clearly defined and constant purpose.

Given this situation, is it reasonable to conduct summative evaluation research? I would argue that it is not appropriate because broad aim programmes have several generalized aims pursued more or less concurrently in situations which are generally unique by the use of non-standardized intervention strategies (see Weiss and Rein, 1970). Summative evaluation in action research programmes fails because in its present form it asks 'does it work', and the translation of the 'it' into the procedure for experimental design requires specific aims pursued by standardized intervention strategies in several situations which can be matched with respect to key variables. Etzioni (1960) rightly states

TABLE 2.3 *Summative evaluation research and action research: key differences*

RESEARCH	
Summation Evaluation	*Action Research*
1. Requires a clear and constant purpose.	1. Tentative, non-committal and adaptive.
2. Logical development of steps.	2. Focused on the next stage.
3. Perceives the present situation in the context of the final outcome.	3. Evolves the future out of emerging opportunities.
4. Is not able to interpret the present until it knows the answer to its ultimate questions.	4. Has to interpret the present as a basis for asking questions.
5. Focuses upon a limited range of factors.	5. Attempts to comprehend a wide range of factors in a dynamic relationship.

Based upon the analysis of community action programmes by Marris and Rein, 1967.

that models of organizational processes which start out with the assumption of goals are intrinsically unsatisfactory. Nearly all studies undertaken with the goal model demonstrate that the goals are not being achieved and that alternative goals are being pursued. Etzioni suggests that goals are sets of meanings for the members of an enterprise which depict target states. In contrast to the target state, real organizations are multi-functional units. It follows that the comparison of an ideal state with an actual state will reveal discrepancies. Such knowledge is not particularly useful because we do not know why the discrepancy exists.

The sources of failure in summative evaluation are in part technical, that is the inability of the experimental design to respond to key issues. Other problems arise from tensions we have observed between the practitioners, evaluators, and sponsors. Major administrative difficulties include the very real possibility that the evaluation group will not know what is going on and will be dependent upon uncommitted record keepers. Also, the existence of the evaluation may impose a premature definition of the goals of the change programme and thus exacerbate the well-known conflicts of activity and interests between themselves and the practitioner. Difficulties rarely arise from the incompetence of the evaluation researcher as a technologist, but rather from the methodological mismatch between the technique and the type of change programme being evaluated.*

The alternative approach starts with the question 'what happened?' and is concerned to collect a wide range of data in order to provide an account of the phases of the project, particularly the development of events through time. The approach aims to obtain coherent accounts of the enterprise before the intervention, of the form taken by the intervention, and of the emerging structures and values which incorporate the intervention. By adopting this approach of formative evaluation, we should be able to identify the interaction between the change programme and the context in which it is introduced, especially the forces which shape the programme, the kinds of opposition encountered, and the unanticipated outcomes.

Formative evaluation requires conceptual frameworks which spell out the range of situations and phenomena that should be included; which reveal the unfolding of the programme with respect to the formation and dissolution of coalitions; which locates the key political processes facilitating and hindering the programme. We shall examine this approach further in Chapter 9.

2.5 Applied research

Applied research is directed towards the solution of a practical problem arising within a sponsoring system by the application of appropriate knowledge. It is undertaken by practitioners who are qualified in one or more of the behavioural sciences. Unlike evaluation research, there is no special reason why the sponsor's definition of the problem would be automatically accepted as specifying the terms of reference. However, in practice it is quite likely that sponsors will only identify the problems for which they believe there are solutions. When applied research is completed it may or may not be written up in report form. This will depend upon the type of sponsoring system and it is quite probable that the great majority of applied work is never written up in reports. When it is, there is very little chance of these being disseminated outside the small circle of people who sponsored and undertook the research.

* For a cogent and contrary view, see D. T. Campbell, 1970.

Occasionally case studies are published in professional journals. Because the feedback is entirely within the sponsoring system those of us in the academic world see very little of the applied work unless we make special excursions to examine its content and utilization. The fact that applied work takes place within the sponsoring system means that it is directed towards a single audience. It is thus typically expressed in the local language and meanings of that audience and hence is not readily comprehended by the outsider coming in for a short visit. The fact of the single audience means that applied work as I have defined it does not readily contribute to basic research, yet the potential is certainly present. Typically, the capability is excluded because of the requirements from sponsors that applied researchers will continue resolving immediate problems on the basis of existing knowledge rather than adding to the total stock of knowledge. For this reason it is quite possible that a practitioner may be applying knowledge which has been shown to be inadequate.

I shall illustrate applied research with two cases from work I did while a member of a large British knitwear firm between 1960 and 1963. The firm had a keen interest in innovation, especially in the training field, and had had an interest in the behavioural sciences for some time. I was the first sociologist that they had recruited for full-time employment. Shortly after I joined, it was suggested that I should assist with the extension of the long-established job description and evaluation scheme from the shopfloor to the clerical, sales, and junior management areas. So I was sent to the British subsidiary of an American plant hire firm to learn about their methods and to assess whether they could be used without modification. Like most young graduates, my approach to the problem included diving off to the local university library to read about job analysis and evaluation. From this reading I learnt that the actual ranking of jobs on the evaluation side tended to be similar irrespective of the number of factors used to compile the points. For example, the American firm I visited had a scheme based upon eight factors yet according to previous research studies they would have had substantially the same results with only three. My other finding related to research on the measurement of responsibility in jobs by Jaques (see J. M. M. Hill, 1958), who divided the content of jobs into prescribed and discretionary and then measured the discretionary content by discovering the length of time between a discretionary decision being made and its being checked. All jobs contain discretionary elements and the length of time that these discretionary elements continue unchecked varies. Jaques selects the longest period for the job-holder and then ranks jobs on the basis of the length of time span of discretion.

I checked opinion on the validity of the research findings by Jaques and discovered that most of the people I consulted were cautious or entirely sceptical, yet it seemed that his method could provide a valuable analytical tool. My view was that many of the managers, though technically proficient, were ill equipped to deal with the organizational problems which would arise with technological and further market changes in the knitwear industry. With this in mind I suggested that we should get the eight-factor scheme from the American firm and choose three crucial factors which would be the main basis for the evaluation. Additionally, we would include a fourth factor – the time span of discretion – in the official evaluation manual, but would not be committed to including it in the final decisions. There was a double advantage from this. First, we could compare the time-span measure and the sum of the score from the other three factors. Second, the use of the time span of discretion in the job analysis and with management would focus attention upon the nature of subordinate's discretion whilst at the same time revealing if the manager actually had a procedure for controlling and checking the subordinate's behaviour. From my point of view this transformed the weak side of the project, namely the job analysis, into a meaningful examination of tasks, of their connectedness, and of their discretionary content. We arranged for members of management to read a short booklet describing the time-span method so that they would benefit from the project; an interesting unanticipated consequence of this was the usual tease about sociology being soft was never heard again.*

My second case is taken from a work study project at a branch factory. This factory was only four years old when I arrived and it had grown from a score of people to about four hundred. During the period of establishment, the work-study function had not been taken very seriously with the consequence, in management's opinion, that the piece rates were loose and layout and methods inadequate. As part of the tightening up on the methods side, management proposed that a group of women examiners should be studied. The women received knitted pieces such as arms and backs in bundles from the male knitters who were the most

---

* Prework is increasingly recognized as essential to the use of the behavioural sciences.

prestigious and cohesive group in the factory. The examiner placed each knitted piece on a table into which a plate of frosted glass had been placed with a light underneath. She then used a Perspex iron to open out the knitted piece to check for faults. This search for faults was difficult, yet its success was important for minimizing imperfect garments at the final stages of manufacture. At the start of the study, the women were working on benches which were open and flat, and they had moved sets of four tables together so that they could talk while working. Management believed that because the women talked there were mistakes, and further, that because each woman's work was piled in bundles on the table and on nearby areas, there was a great likelihood of pieces from different dyes being mixed. The solution? Building each woman a table with shelves all around for piling the work up, and place the tables in a line so that the women could not talk so easily.

My studies of the method and the timings indicated that there was no good case for making this change. More important, a close observation of the organization of the work indicated that the women made hardly any mistakes, and that they always knew where their work was located. Also, they were able to exchange pieces within a group of four tables to make up complete bundles for the next stage, thus reducing the problems of coordination. I have mentioned that detecting faults was difficult, yet there was no formal training and each new worker learnt on the job from an unofficial leader. Finally, it was clear from my observations that the women formed a cohesive group. I had noted that they would speak to the knitters about imperfect work. My interpretation was that in the existing system the women were able to learn the job quickly, were soon located in a cohesive work group which could sustain its interpretation of the quality standard by virtue of its cohesion against the social pressures of the knitters to be more lax in areas where discretion was high. In effect, we had what has been described in the social science literature as an autonomous work group, one which regulates and controls its own tasks. The researches of E. L. Trist, of A. K. Rice, and others indicated that the autonomous group was functional in certain specified conditions and I considered this to be one such condition and recommended the continuance of the existing system. This was rejected. The majority of the trained hands left or requested transfer, and when management's new system was introduced it required the appointment of a supervisor/trainer and pushed up the unit cost.

c

The two cases I have selected represent applications from existing knowledge. The end products have been written about here for the first time. They are of little interest as such to basic researchers because a number of key requirements of the research design are absent, but they do illustrate some of the features of applied work for, in this case, the sociologist. In this applied work I used the findings from researches on the factors in job evaluation schemes, on the time span of discretion and from autonomous groups, but this was not connected to the work of scientists and hence any potential general relevance of the findings would be lost. Although these particular examples have no long-term relevance, the same firm provided the setting in which I started to rethink some of the problems involved in organizational change (see P. A. Clark, 1972, pp. 39–41). At that time it was necessary to leave industry and take a research appointment in order to explore these ideas further, and this points to the importance of flexibility and the potential role of the universities at this early stage of behavioural science application.

2.6 Action research

Action research has three task masters: the sponsor, the behavioural science practitioner, and the scientific community. The fact that these dissimilar groups are related for the duration of a project imposes many strains, and it must be observed that one of the major problems facing the action researcher is the devising of appropriate administrative mechanisms for simultaneously linking and separating these groups. E. Litwak's observations on the importance of segregating and insulating dissimilar forms of social organization are especially relevant for successful action research (see Litwak, 1961, R. K. Merton, 1957).

Action research is one strategy for influencing the stock of knowledge of the sponsoring enterprise. In that sense, it is a strategy for distributing knowledge, but the ideal project is one in which both the behavioural scientists and the sponsors benefit through having a better understanding of a particular problem. Typically, the sponsors are concerned to ensure that they 'get value for money spent', and hence not always especially concerned with the theoretical activities and interests of practitioners.

Action research is also concerned with adding to the stock of knowledge of scientists and is said to be a way of gaining 'privileged access' to data and situations which are normally not easily accessible to the basic researcher. There it *can* make important contributions to theory.

A definition of action research adopted from R. Rapoport has been chosen because it addresses the problems which Sanford referred to as central to the constructive development of action research. Rapoport formulates his definition thus:

Action research aims to contribute *both* to the practical concerns of people in an immediate problematic situation and to the goals of social science by joint collaboration within a mutually acceptable ethical framework.

The importance of Rapoport's definition is that it draws a sharp distinction between applied and action research. The former is not concerned to enlarge the stock of knowledge of the social science community, merely to use what exists. Rapoport further states:

Action research is a type of applied social research differing from other varieties in the immediacy of the researcher's involvement in the action process.

The fact of 'immediacy' is in many ways obvious, but what is less clear is the *direction* to be taken by the behavioural scientist during the involvement.

M. Foster, a senior member of a leading research institute, the Tavistock Institute of Human Relations, London, suggests that we should specify more precisely the linkage between the researchers and the creation of an organizational change. He would add a further sentence to Rapoport's definition:

... and the intention of the parties is to be involved in change [which must be] change involving the properties of the system itself.*

Thus action research must possess an aspect of direct involvement in organizational change, and simultaneously it must provide an increase in knowledge. F. Heller suggests that there are two principal ways in which this can occur. First, when there can be an attempt to test out and/or replicate theory in a new setting by immediate involvement in the implementation phase of a situation which constitutes a valid test of the theory. Second, by joining a situation in which a decision about

---

* Instances of structural change of the system are rare. Foster cites the work of E. Miller and A. K. Rice, P. A. Clark and A. B. Cherns, in Britain, and S. Seashore and D. Bowers in North America as significant examples.

action has been taken by members of the sponsoring system. The role of the practitioner is to document the change process and provide feedback on the organizational change process so that it might be stopped, modified, or accelerated. Heller observes that helping with the implementation of changes is optional, but in terms of the definition of action research I have adopted throughout this book it is essential that the practitioner be involved.

It follows from our definition that we are concerned with developmental work rather than routinized activities. This would suggest that action research will be typified by an essentially fluid relationship between the practitioner and the client. In instances where the problem definition is general and subject to redefinition, and the 'raw material' (i.e. the problem) of the action research is full of exceptions and judgemental search processes, then the relationships would be typified by loose and changing definitions of roles (Perrow, 1970). Our argument draws upon the contingency theorists' analysis of tasks and structure to arrive at a conclusion which is somewhat similar to that reached for different reasons by Bennis.

Action research is distinguished by its special requirements in research methodology. I would argue that the strategy for gaining the utilization of the research has to be integrated with the research design at the start of the project. This requires the practitioner to devote considerable time to the creation of an infrastructure for receiving the findings and acting upon them. These considerations are central to practice, and may lead, as Gouldner observes, to carrying out activities which appear to be scientifically senseless, but are designed to provide insight. Thus the 'rules of the game' in action research differ sharply from those adopted in presenting papers to colleagues in the scientific community – even allowing for the idealized notions of how this is actually undertaken (see Merton, 1957; Haagstrom, 1966; Kuhn, 1970).

Summary

We approach the subject matter of action research best by recognizing that there are several different ways in which the term 'research' is currently used. The typology, based on the dimensions of problem orientation, channel of diffusion, and number of relevant audiences, assisted in the highlighting of the important differences between five kinds of research.

We noted that the dominant existing type undertaken for sponsors is evaluation research which highlighted the symbols of measurement and scientific neutrality but minimized the influence of the behavioural science perspective, except in the instance of formative evaluation. Evaluation research of the summative kind is frequently used to attempt to assess change programmes, but I have argued that its relevance is restricted by its technology and assumptions.

The use of the behavioural sciences to tackle problems in organizations owes its existence to applied and action research. The latter is distinguished from the former by its concern to create organizational change and simultaneously study the process. To achieve this objective requires a careful division of labour within those agencies undertaking action research, but we shall look at this problem through the successive chapters and tackle the main snags in Chapter 11.

CHAPTER 3

Organizational change approaches

The planning of organizational change by making use of existing plus specially acquired knowledge about organizational behaviour in general, and the situation in a sponsoring system in particular, is a phenomenon of the past decade, and one which is rapidly increasing. In this chapter our first aim is to find the variety of intervention points which practitioners can operate in order to facilitate change. Generally speaking, there has been a tendency for practitioners to concentrate upon one of the following four variables: task, technology, structure, and people. It is argued that these variables are in fact highly interdependent, and therefore change approaches should seek to operate across them. Also it may be possible to achieve change in, for example, the people variable, indirectly by changing aspects of the technology.* Therefore I shall argue that our study of organizational change must recognize the possibility of both multiple points of intervention in the sponsoring system and also the advantage of indirect change.

Multiple points of intervention raises the crucial issue of problem territories, by which is meant the division of labour within academic disciplines in the educational system and that within enterprises between the professional associations. The topic of problem territories is introduced and further illustrated in the case studies and ensuing analysis. It may be noted that by isolating the problem territories of particular approaches we can detect consistent patterns linking their territorial claim with specific methods. This suggests that some of the controversies between the methods of achieving change do, in effect, arise from different aims.

Approaches to organizational change are becoming increasingly formalized and packaged. Frequently academics are critical of packaged solutions, but this neglects the very important possibilities which these methods can present for problems that are frequently encountered. Formalization may take place in both the diagnostic phases, as in the

---

* L. E. Davis and J. C. Taylor, 1972, have provided a strong case backed by extensive research to substantiate this point.

development of core questionnaires by Seashore and colleagues at the Institute of Social Research, Ann Arbor, Michigan. The aim of the core questionnaire is to make a microprobe of the state of the social system, and the technology has been developed to the point where results can be obtained within six weeks of the probe.* Similarly, Beckhard (1967) has developed a one-day method which he calls the Confrontation Meeting. Formalization may also occur in the solution phase. In this chapter we shall examine one formalized approach tackling essentially the people variable. This is the Managerial Grid.

3.1 Points for intervention

Organizational change as a deliberate activity requires a theory to guide the selection of points of intervention within the sponsoring system. Attempts to change organizations by changing individuals through teaching have been heavily criticized and currently practitioners stress the importance of developing approaches that are focused upon the whole organization as a functioning entity. Planned organizational change proceeds .by identifying and manipulating those variables which are most readily controlled and the identification of the

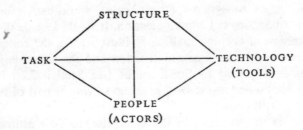

FIGURE 1

key variables requires the application of an organizational perspective of the kind suggested by H. Leavitt who starts from the observation that there are a wide range of perspectives and suggests that a classification can be constructed by viewing organizations as multivariate systems within which there are four salient interacting variables, as in Figure 1 (from Leavitt in Cooper *et al.*, 1964).

* Communication from J. C. Taylor.

Task refers to the objectives of the organization. For example, the objectives of an American pyjama firm, Weldon, prior to their takeover by Harwood, was to manufacture for a high-class market. After the takeover the task was changed to manufacturing for the general market (see Marrow *et al.*, 1967). Leavitt intends the definition to include the large variety of different but operationally significant sub-tasks that exist in major enterprises. In the military, for instance, units have many subsidiary tasks. An airfield might have to be on permanent standby as a point of arrival for civil aircraft in an emergency situation. The existence of this task implies that there will be a replication of some of the facilities that exist on civil airfields (see Section 4.5).

Technology refers to equipment, plant, and buildings. Leavitt is inclined to include problem-solving inventions, such as work study, and is consequently uncertain about the distinction between technology and structure; I propose to restrict my usage to raw materials, machine technology, its spatial and temporal configurations.* Changes in technology might arise indirectly from changes in task or directly through improved methods of production. Either way, they might directly affect people and structure. Additionally, the existence of one form of technology tends to restrict the range of tasks an enterprise can undertake.

Structure refers to systems of authority, workflow, information systems, coordination, and communication. It would include the extent of centralization of decision making as illustrated in the comparisons between craft organization in construction and the situation in mass production as described by Stinchcombe (see Section 2.2). I would include the established methods of problem solving as part of structure (see Perrow, 1970).

People refers to the actors in the enterprise, to their attitudes and expectations. We might expect, for example, from researches undertaken on the life cycle that the expectations that people have of work will change in an approximate relationship with age and the state of family responsibilities. Thus men in their youth might be prepared to accept work which they found intrinsically boring in exchange for high earnings, whilst later they might prefer to reverse this relationship. Thus changes in the people variable could affect the capability of an enterprise to adjust to changes in its task, technology, or structure.

---

* See the usage by Pugh and colleagues and his extensive examination of the influence of technology upon structure.

Leavitt states that these four variables are highly interdependent so that a change in one will almost certainly elicit change in the others; however, he observes that each may be thought of as having an associated change strategy.

The approach to the technological variables is essentially that of the production engineer working upon improvements in machine performance and work flow; the operational research analyst applying, for example, linear programming techniques to optimize the relationships between production cost and customer requirements; and the management consultant advising on methods of warehouse storage. The late Joan Woodward commented: 'Every time a production engineer makes a decision about such matters as batch size he influences the pattern of relationships on the shop-floor' (Woodward, 1964), and this comment points to the recent interest of behaviourial scientists in the activities of those exponents adopting the technological approach. If this statement of the causal relationship can be demonstrated, then clearly it is possible to alter the social system indirectly by manipulating the technical system. It should be noted that Woodward uses the term 'influence' and does not specify the direction, hence it would not be reasonable to suggest that she is advocating technological determinism, but rather is hinting at ways in which established social groupings may be affected by changes in technological variables (see Trist, 1963; Touraine, 1965; Sadler and Barry, 1970).

The structuralist approach contains several conflicting schools of thought about organizational change. The classical stance emphasizes defining the areas of responsibility and enforcing the chain of command as a means of change. In contrast, contemporary exponents tend to emphasize decentralization of responsibility to work centres which are responsible for a defined set of activities. The tasks people do are modified by altering the over-all features of such aspects as cost control. More recently, a small number of practitioners have modified the flow of work and the arrangement of people, focusing upon activities and interactions as points of change facilitating changes in values where required (see Chapple and Sayles, 1961; P. A. Clark, 1972).

The people approaches try to change organizations by changing the behaviour of the actors as a means of achieving changes in the structure and effectiveness. This approach dominates the organizational change literature and practice. The original manipulative approaches exemplified by *How to Win Friends and Influence People* was replaced after

1945 by Lewin's emphasis upon involvement and group pressure as means of achieving change. More recently still there has been a sharper awareness, especially amongst the social psychologists who developed this approach, that group pressure was a form of manipulation which did not deal with the key issue of the power structure of the enterprise. Thus power equalization between sponsor and practitioner is now advocated. However, even this does not adequately face the problem in whose interest is organizational change. Further, although power equalization approaches criticize alternatives on the grounds of hidden economic costs, there is in fact no satisfactory confirmation to date that one is more economical than the other.

The value of Leavitt's formulation of the salient interacting variables is that it suggests the possibilities for multiple points of entry to achieve organizational change. For example, a careful examination of the account by Marrow and colleagues of Harwood's takeover of Weldon shows not only the radical changes in the task mentioned earlier but also in the layout, raw materials, number and responsibilities of supervision. Bearing in mind Leavitt's scheme and the usual difficulties of achieving organizational change, especially of the dramatic kind as at Weldon, it may be seen that the changes occurred in all probability because of the multiple sources of change rather than from work on the people variable (see Seashore and Bowers, 1964).

Although the scheme suggests to the practitioner that there are a variety of perspectives and sources of change, it does not tackle the problem of deciding the relative strength of one as set against another. This limitation is recognized by Leavitt, whose principle objective is to map the existing approaches to organizational change, to highlight their partial nature, and *to suggest that in the future we should be less committed to the use of only single points of intervention*. Ideally, approaches to organizational change should take account of the possibilities presented by the four interacting variables to create multiple points of intervention.

3.2 Problem territories

Who owns problems? This apparently simple question raises many of the underlying issues in approaches to action research as a strategy for organizational change. We tend to think of problems as being owned by particular disciplines in universities and by specialisms in enterprises, yet if we look more closely it is apparent that ownership is always subject to change. The fact of ownership and the ability of one group to retain the ownership of significant problems strongly determines the growth of professional associations.

In Chapter 2 we noted that in certain kinds of research the problem is owned by one set of actors. Thus problems in basic research are owned by scientists, and in evaluation research by the sponsors. Action research is distinctive because the sponsor's problem presents an opportunity to the scientist and the practitioner to resolve problems arising in their separate fields. Organizational change, as a field of enquiry, cuts across the traditional disciplinary boundaries in the universities and colleges, and, equally significant, it cuts across the boundaries of existing professional associations. For example, operational researchers attempting to maximize the flow of orders through an enterprise may devise a solution which has dysfunctional consequences for the social system. In fact, leading operational researchers in the United Kingdom became aware of this possibility in the early 1960s and organized a series of conferences to identify areas of collaboration (see J. R. Lawrence, 1967). An interesting feature of the proposed collaboration was the expectation from operational researchers that the behavioural scientist was only competent to facilitate the installation of their solutions. This expectation may be seen as entirely justifiable when we note that behavioural scientists have tended to claim planned organizational change as a territory but ignored the equally relevant topic of what was to be introduced. I have suggested earlier that we should be concerned with organizational design and hence should influence the selection of the solution to be implemented.

In the previous section we noted the separate nature of existing change approaches. This indicates that each approach represents ownership of a problem territory and raises the important question, What are the possibilities for organizational change approaches that cross professional boundaries? Even more difficult to ascertain is the likely behaviour of sponsors faced by competing professionals claiming the same problem.

The answer to the question who owns problems is complex and it is clear that the existing patterns of ownership are important. Action research, to be successful in navigating through the territories of various professional associations, requires a special language to facilitate cooperation. We shall examine this further in Chapter 6.

3.3   Formalization

The case studies in the next chapter indicate wide variations in the extent to which the activities of the practitioner were formalized. This is an important aspect of intervention strategies and it has considerable implications for the development and diffusion of new practices (see Sections 12.2 and 12.3).

Social inventions such as the Managerial Grid, and certain types of curriculum reform in education, are highly formalized in both the diagnosis and the implementation of the solution. It is convenient to examine the topic by adapting Bowers' distinction (1970) between diagnostic and solution phases and between the use of instrumented technologies or self in either or both of these. These two dimensions combine to provide a fourfold scheme:

		Intervention Method	
		PERSONALIZED	INSTRUMENTED
Phase of organiza- tional change	DIAGNOSTIC	A	C
	SOLUTION	B	D

Based on Bowers, 1970.

A represents a situation in which the diagnostic stage is conducted by the practitioner using a qualitative assessment of the situation (see Paterson, Section 4.5).

B is illustrated in two studies: Hjelholt (Section 4.3) uses interpretation of conference material to assist shipping crews and associated shore personnel involved in inducting technologically advanced tankers to Danish shipping lines; Paterson uses his own role to subtly introduce changes within the flying members of the aerodrome.

C represents an attempt to establish more objective data as the basis of diagnosis. It is illustrated by the development work done in the creation of core questionnaires by Seashore (see Bowers, 1970), and by Chartrand (1972) in Canadian public bureaucracies.

D is illustrated by such technologies as the Managerial Grid (see next Section).

The development of an instrumented technology for tackling probably reflects two important influences. First, an increasing demand for applied research has given a small number of persons a great deal of practical experience which they have utilized to create systematic means for tackling specific organizational changes. Second, some sponsors, the large enterprises for example, have a culture in which there are strong preferences for apparently objective and impersonal technologies for tackling social and human problems.

3.4 Social inventions: the Managerial Grid (R. Blake and J. S. Mouton)

With the growth of the uses of the behavioural sciences in solving organizational problems there has also occurred a parallel development in the creation of general solutions to widely experienced problems. The best known examples of this are contained within an approach known as organizational development. Within this school there has been a growth of systemic approaches at the level of the group and at the level of the whole organization. One of the best-known examples of an organizational approach is that of the Managerial Grid.

We shall use the term 'social inventions' to refer to the Grid and to similar solutions such as confrontation meetings, autonomous groups, job enrichment, and System 4 type of participative management. These inventions are characterized by a relatively high degree of formalization. Before examining the Managerial Grid we shall briefly note the general aims of those exponents who are located within the organizational development school. Typically, they emphasize the people variable rather than task, technology, or structure. Their aim is to achieve change in one or more of three areas: interpersonal relations, intergroup relations, interdepartmental relations. Generally speaking, organizational development at the group level uses various forms of group experience, both unstructured as in sensitivity training and structured as in the task-oriented exercises devised by Coverdale and pioneered in Esso.

Bennis and colleagues have stated that the coordination of almost every contemporary human organization is achieved by the social invention known as 'bureaucracy',* and that the strength of this mode

---

* The utility of the concept of bureaucracy has been challenged severely by the work of Pugh, Hickson, and colleagues (1968, 1969). Albrow (1970), in a careful appraisal of the origins of the concept and its usage in the European literature,

of organizing is its capacity to manage efficiently that which is routine and predictable in human affairs. This observation on contemporary society is central to an understanding of the selection of attitudes as the point of focus, the collaborative relationship with sponsors and subjects, and the use of group decision methods as the intervention strategy. He suggests that bureaucracy was appropriate to the exigencies of the Industrial Revolution and the particular problems of an enterprise like the railways, but argues that the key defining feature of contemporary society is change, not stability. The environments of enterprises are said to be characterized by increased interdependence, increased turbulence, and an increase in the number of complex long-term projects (cf. Schon, 1970). Consequently the tasks of organizations will become more technical, complicated and unprogrammed. The key organizational concept becomes 'temporary' and the need for innovation will be within the enterprise itself. Existing social institutions will not be able to withstand, let alone cope with, such a devastating rate of change without basic alterations in the way in which they conduct their core activities and negotiate their environments. Bennis suggests that the enterprise of the future will require persons of very diverse, highly specialized competence. Hence the central question becomes, How can we devise an organizational structure capable of coping with change and providing a configuration of relationships and values that can maintain persons with diverse outlooks within the same organizational framework? The difficulty is said to be made greater because new entrants to the bureaucracies possess values that conflict with those of established members. Bennis believes that managers are already adapting; interestingly, he argues that it is the managers who are *leading* the shift in values within the major enterprises, and that the academics are following this trend. To emphasize the point he suggests that the popularity of McGregor's writing and seminars is based upon his rare empathy for managers. The shift in values from dominant styles of managership and to greater emphasis upon persuasion has been commented upon by M. Janowitz (1960) with reference to the military in America, and M. Crozier (1964) with reference to the industrial enterprise in Europe.

---

suggests that the concept as generally used is so ill-defined that it should be abandoned. Kohn (1971) points out that there is a tendency for men who work in bureaucratic organizations to be more intellectually flexible, more open to new experience, more self-directed, than men in non-bureaucratic organizations.

The exponents of organizational development present it as a response to changes in organizational ideologies about authority in a period of change. Organizational development is a complex educational strategy that attempts to change attitudes, beliefs, and indirectly alter the structure of enterprises so that they have a greater capacity for coping with change. The focus is upon the people variable, especially values and organizational climates, as the point of entry rather than upon task, structure and technology. It relies on change in climate, especially the degree of openness in interpersonal relationships, in authority patterns and risk taking. Bennis presents several examples to illustrate its experimental emphasis and to stress that it cannot be sufficiently understood if it is regarded only as sensitivity training. The examples are:

- Team development (for example, individual executives complete short questionnaires on key dimensions of executive performance. The answers are pooled, given priorities, and fed back to the group as the basis for discussion)
- Inter-group conflict
- Confrontation meetings
- Data feedback

The most widely known example of the systemic change strategy is the Managerial Grid devised by Blake and Mouton,* who consider that it is applicable, with small modifications, in a wide variety of situations including education, hospitals, the military and industry. The aim of the Grid is to replace both evolutionary and revolutionary approaches to organizational change by a systemic development which is defined as the planned design of concepts and strategies. The chosen point of intervention is the leaders of autonomous (non-interdependent) units. These may be sub-units of a large enterprise or they may involve the entire enterprise; it is assumed that influence exerted at the top will lead to further change at other levels. In application, the Grid is in part a do-it-yourself kit, in which selected company men play key roles in the implementation of the programme, which might take several years. During this period the managers are in part learning by doing, and this learning is an aspect of the revitalization of the enterprise.

The application of the whole strategy may be considered in six phases,

* Blake and Mouton have written cogently and extensively on the objectives and theoretical basis of their work. The key sources are contained in the references.

starting with laboratories* conducted off the site and ending with more focused laboratories involving working groups on the site. The first stages include the identification of the areas of excellence, the collection of data from managers on the extent to which objectives are achieved, the feedback of the pooled findings and their discussion in terms of managerial styles. This focus upon managerial styles rather than inter-personal relations distinguishes the Managerial Grid from sensitivity training.

Excellence is defined as 'what should be' in relation to 'what is'. The strategy is therefore to discover 'what is' and 'what should be' by having the members of the group complete questionnaires referring to key areas of performance. These are completed both singly and as a working group. Each of the major functions (e.g. finance, operating and marketing) is evaluated in terms of current effectiveness, flexibility, and potential for development. There are six functions which are evaluated in terms of these three criteria, thereby giving 18 boxes. Each box is then assessed for 'orientation'. Orientations are classed along two-dichotomized dimensions:

> defensive / aggressive
> internal / external

and are combined to give an assessment (e.g. internal/aggressive). The combination of orientations with the functions and the three areas provides data on a wide variety of actual organizational behaviour. This strategy is devised to make concepts come alive in operational terms.† Blake has formulated the six-stage programme, each phase of which is highly developed in its procedures and administration for tackling problems which managers have identified as major barriers to effective performance.

The application aims to improve creative thinking by educating managers about basic social processes. In addition, basic concepts aid the manager to diagnose the organization and anticipate difficulties. The first three phases of the Grid concentrate upon problems of communication. Participants start by reading the learning theories at seminars and then proceed by applying them in team and interteam

* This is the term used by practitioners to describe the meetings at which they interact with managers.

† Each member is required to complete approximately 40 hours pre-work of selected reading before attending.

exercises. In these three stages the Grid is introduced and learnt. The Grid may be thought of as having two dimensions. One represents a concern for people, and the other a concern for completing the task; both are scored on a nine-point scale. Combining the two dimensions provides 81 positions of which 5 are initially identified: 1·1; 1·9; 5·5; 9·1; and 9·9. The Grid represents managerial styles. The members of the team complete questionnaires which are scored and then translated into positions on the Grid. Blake suggests that the 9·9 style (that is, highly task and people oriented) is widely identified by managers as the soundest way to achieve excellence. In the communication seminars the manager learns to recognize his own style and that of others through a mixture of projects and formalized self-evaluation procedures. The results of this also provide the consultant with the basis of many diagnostic insights into the problems and culture of the company. Although the first stages focus upon communication, they also tackle conflict, commitment, and creativity.

In the second half of the Grid the three phases are concerned with planning. The executives develop an ideal strategic model for the organization and scrutinize it to see how it can be implemented and evaluated. Blake argues that 'corporate excellence' is achieved when the culture commits people to solving organizational problems. The Grid is based upon the premise that the management of conflict and emotions will significantly influence organizational performance, and that the open discussion of differences in interpersonal styles within the enterprise is crucial. The ultimate goal of this approach is to develop the organization. Hence it is focused upon groups from within the client enterprise, and the leadership for the Grid is provided, in part, from within.

Summary

In this chapter we have examined four aspects of organizational change. First, it is argued that approaches to change must view the organization as a whole and pinpoint the potential for change within the interacting variables of task, technology, structure, and people. Second, to attempt to achieve this involves crossing the existing boundaries of problem ownership within the academic system, within the sponsoring system, and between them. Third, existing approaches to widely experienced problems can be formalized so that a general diagnostic and solution

D

technology can be created. Fourth, the Managerial Grid illustrates the possibilities of formalization. It shows that a change technology dealing with the people variable is a lengthy process.

Each aspect raises distinct problems. First, how can we improve the Leavitt scheme and identify in theoretical terms the sources of organizational change? Second, how can we create problem-solving situations where existing professional and academic boundaries can be made more flexible? Third, how do we learn more about the process of formalizing and developing social inventions? Fourth, how do we learn how to identify the problems to which these formalized social inventions can be applied, and how do we decide whether an application is feasible?

Each of these aspects is represented in the case studies contained in the next chapter, and each is analysed further in the chapters that follow.

CHAPTER 4

Case studies

Applied social science has, in effect, become one of the
planned functional substitutes for the spontaneous adaptive
mechanisms by means of which the rational organization
responds to external threats. A. W. GOULDNER

In this chapter we present seven accounts of organizational change,
showing a variety of points of intervention and methods of changing.
In each case the reader should note the characteristics of the problem;
who the practitioners were; the relationship between the practitioner
and sponsor with particular reference to the relative influence of each
upon problem definition and the development of the project; the
methods of diagnosis used by the practitioner and the extent to which
the findings were shared with the sponsor; the ways in which data were
presented to the sponsor; the context of the project with particular
respect to the subculture in which it was undertaken; the sponsor's
expectations and feelings of urgency about the problem and confidence
with the practitioner; the availability of resources of time and money
to solve the problem.

The case studies have been selected as a whole to bring out the main
themes and patterns. Individual cases will tend to emphasize some
aspects rather than others. For example, those from shipping, the
military, and hospitals include a brief introduction to the distinctive
subcultural features, whilst the study of job enrichment emphasizes the
role of one sponsor in creating an instrumented technology for tackling
problems of job design.

The analysis of the case studies will be presented in the chapters that
follow.

4.1 Organizational renewal in hospitals (R. W. Revans)

This study was undertaken at ten hospitals in Great Britain; it represents an innovative form of action research with great possibilities for
development and wider application. Two special features of this
example should be noted: the distinctive aspects of the health service

in the U.K.; the theories of R. W. Revans with regard to organizational learning.

In 1947 the National Health Act was passed by Parliament, heralding the introduction of a public medical service. A private sector would continue, but the majority of the population could have free access to medical services. The operation, planning, financing, and evaluation of the hospital service is now undertaken at a national level. Within the hospitals a high proportion of beds are allocated to non-fee-paying persons, attended by doctors and nurses who are, like university lecturers, full-time public servants paid from funds raised by taxation. However, consultants may operate within both the public and private sectors, thus there is a continuance of pre-1947 features into the new service. The major differences between the British and North American medical care systems are well-known, so we shall concentrate upon those elements which are central to understanding the work associated with the initiatives of Revans.

Hospitals are distinguished from manufacturing and commercial enterprises by the fact that they are people processing, which means that the internal procedures must attract and motivate the members. In the case of hospitals some of the members (the patients) are temporary, hence the importance of length of stay as a measure of performance. Hospitals are expected to provide a service, not to engage in market transactions. Historically, they have been associated with the church and the military, and normally they do not have single lines of authority but contain three interdependent subcultures. For example, nurses are semi-professionals, their activities being directed by senior nurses. The patterns of authority in the ward tend to be formal in contrast to the operating theatre (Coser, 1956). Also it may be noted that professional workers constitute the line personnel. Associated with this is that the break between the technical and managerial levels (Parsons, 1960) occurs at a high level in the organizational unit. Finally, the organizational structure must be able to cope with emergencies, it must have certain elements of flexibility.

Revans has considerable research experience in two public sectors, mining and hospitals. In researches on labour turnover and absenteeism in the collieries of the National Coal Board, he identified factors influencing the level of morale. Later, he completed studies of morale within the hospitals. From the latter studies Revans postulated a causal connection between the patient's length of stay in hospital and the state of morale among nursing and medical members of the staff (Revans, 1962). He suggested that where the precise nature of a patient's illness was not known, the key decision makers – the doctors and consultants – were dependent for an adequate analysis upon small pieces of information from the nurses. The nurses were in the position of almost continuous surveillance, whilst the doctors and consultants were only present for short periods, and the passing of vital information to the doctor depended on the perceptions of appropriate behaviour within the highly hierarchized nursing staff, and between them and the doctors. If the nurses felt that they could not communicate their observations, then the doctor had to judge on a small amount of information. The patient feels anxious in such a situation. As Revans puts it; 'Hospitals are institutions cradled in anxiety.' This anxiety is enhanced by uncertainty, and the uncertainty magnified by failures. The result is that the average patient stay in low morale hospitals is greater than in high morale hospitals. The linking by Revans of performance and morale with regard to hospitals is in no way compromised by recent critical assessments of the morale-performance theory. Revans circulated the findings of his studies (examples of basic objective research) through learned journals, professional and 'trade' journals, and through popular journalism. He also wrote a short and highly factual account of his studies specifically for persons working in hospitals (Revans, 1964). At this stage he considered that he had defined a problem area of crucial relevance – the communication system – and now was the moment to do something about changing the existing situation.

Though Revans defined a key problem area he deliberately did not propose a specific solution (Revans, 1967). Instead, he suggested that the problem of communication could be solved best by those working within the hospitals. In this formulation, the role of the behavioural scientist is to assist with the technology of data collection and analysis. Revans argues that an organizational change programme should be guided by the 'maximum of practice and the minimum of theory', and that theory should consist of the study of action research projects in parallel fields. This observation reflects his theory of learning in organizations. In essence, this states that the members of organizations are willing to work and do seek self-development, hence they are intimately concerned about training and are consequently dependent upon communication and feedback. Revans argues that learning and living are so interdependent that we should design living to facilitate learning. From these arguments he then suggests that the traditional model of carrying out research is of little value to the administrator. His concept is that the managers should collect their own data and that the hospitals should be encouraged to develop their own models of learning and change.

In 1965 the King Edward VII Hospital Fund began to play an important role in supporting a programme of action research related to the problems identified by Revans. With financial encouragement from the Ministry of Health, a programme of 'institutional learning' was established in a self-selected sample of ten London hospitals. Revans had deliberately decided not to tell the hospitals how they should organize themselves, and merely pointed out that morale and communications were important in this context. He suggested that senior persons should attend short courses in research techniques and then return to their hospitals to assist in instituting a series of internally formulated projects directed towards actual problems in the hospital. In this way Revans hoped to break the 'normal' natural history of a problem: typically, a problem emerges, is defined, and then allocated to experts who apply a procedure for its solution, thereby taking over the 'ownership' of the problem and inhibiting others from learning. In contrast, the medium through which hospital members were to learn more about their own and other persons' roles was through projects selected and undertaken by each hospital. It was expected that both the project and the result would contribute to the learning process. Here we see Revans's theory of education in action. The focus is upon the internal team, and the aim is to avoid the situation in which the external expert 'is bound to be seen by those in charge of the system as a threat to their institutionalized power' (Revans, 1967). The approach is essentially non-directive. At the start of the programme each of the ten hospitals sent three senior members, one from each main group – administrative, nursing, and medical – to a three-day intensive course. Then each of their subordinates attended a one-month course emphasizing the importance of using the correct techniques for data collection in problem solving. It was planned that this course would have a major influence upon the nature of the projects undertaken, but there was a 'minimum of theory'. After the course they returned to their own hospitals and were encouraged to develop their own projects.

The design of the 'experiment' recognized that the concept of the projects was precarious, not least because the principle catalysts in the hospitals had no recognizable role-models to assist them. It was decided that this problem could be eased by arranging periodic meetings at which the project teams from the ten hospitals exchanged experiences. In addition they could gain special kinds of assistance and technical support from a 'Central Team' residing in London. Some of the hospitals employed undergraduate students to help in the collection and analysis of data. The Central Team comprised persons with a variety of skills and special experiences. They were not essentially academic in orientation, since this was not appropriate to the success of the concept. They did not control and direct, but acted as additional resources, working in part by establishing relationships with particular hospitals. It might be asked; Who were the main agents of organizational change? Revans suggests that the Central Team was the primary change agent.

Within the ten hospitals the types of project formulated by the six-person teams varied widely, as did the influence of the teams. In practice they were not always integrated, and in the opinion of one student member, the whole exercise 'lacked skill and knowledge of the social sciences' (Earnshaw, 1969).

An interesting facet of the project was the formation of a team to evaluate the impact of the 'experiment'. This is one of the few examples of action research in which there was concurrent observation and analysis. The evaluation did begin slightly after the start of the project (Wieland and Leigh, 1972), but despite certain difficulties endemic in this kind of work, it proceeded to completion.

4.2 Structural reorganization in insurance (J. J. O'Connell)

This particular study is of considerable interest because it describes the activities of internationally known management consultants who were called in to advise a long-established American insurance company with assets of more than 10 billion dollars and approximately 30,000 employees. It served some 20 million policy holders from its centralized head office and several hundred branch offices. In 1960, the company established a top-level management committee to examine the position of the assistant manager in the branch offices. A senior member of the committee began a dialogue with the management consultants, who sensed that the problem was symptomatic of deeper problems and proposed a diagnostic study. This began in mid-1961.

In the diagnostic phase the consultants interviewed senior personnel at the head office and at the regional level; they examined existing reports on performance, committee minutes, and similar data. They observed meetings and spent two days each at a sample of twenty-two branch offices. The focus of the study was to improve the marketing operation of the company and was thus in part concerned with Leavitt's task variable.

The consultants then began a close examination of the assistant branch manager's role. Each office had a branch manager who was responsible for the over-all performance of the agents, the clerical-administrative workers, and the assistant branch managers (ABMS). The consultants' analysis provided a composite picture of the assistant branch manager – he was in a staff relationship to the agents; he spent 75 per cent of his time with them in assignments known as demonstration selling, but in effect he combined demonstrating to customers with teaching the agents and boosting sales. The remaining time was largely spent in the office processing reports, answering mail, and writing progress reports. This pattern was modified by the monthly and annual peaks.*

In practice, the consultants discovered that almost 85 per cent of the assistant branch manager's time was with agents, either in the field or back at the office. The ABMS were essentially supersalesmen who viewed their jobs as stepping stones to other jobs and other firms in the insurance field.†

The consultants had agreed that the diagnostic study should lead to specific recommendations. Before examining these, three aspects of the ABMS' situation, shaping their activities and behaviour, should be taken into account. First, the environment is one of increased market competition between a variety of types of service for the increasing proportion of savings that became available after 1945. For fifteen years the pro-

---

* For an analysis of the importance of peak periods to organized change, see my forthcoming analysis based on field researches in industry and retail. Theoretical leads arise in Allport's notion of a stream of events, Parsons's work with Shils and Bales on the phase hypothesis, and Etzioni's exposition of the successive division of compliance.

† O'Connell, while carrying out his research on the consultants, also undertook observational studies in two selected branches. Comparison of his findings with that of the consultants suggests that the latter tended to underestimate the amount of unprogrammed activity. While this aspect is of technical relevance, we shall concentrate upon the consultants' work.

ductivity of the agent remained constant and the selling method was the same type of face-to-face approach that had been in operation since before 1900. Second, the structure of authority and rewards imposed certain shaping influences upon the ABMS' activities. For example, the flow of work and information from the agents was directly to the clerical staff and only rarely involved the ABM. Third, the behaviour of the actors was relevant. The branch manager was office-based, regarding himself as responsible for the whole show and having strong feelings about the value of forced savings. He undertook the analysis of performance, kept records, observed the agents, encouraged, criticized, and corrected. He was the first point of call for agents seeking support. The agents tended to exclude the ABMS from peer groups and were strongly involved in personal competition, regarding the ABM as someone who would boost their sales when an assignment arose. In effect they viewed the ABM as a supersalesman and were somewhat cynical about the job.

Of these three sets of variables the environmental set affected the ABM indirectly and was not controllable (see Section 5.1); the structural and behavioural variables were more important and the structural variable was the most open to manipulation.

Once patterns began to emerge from the diagnosis, the consultants began the oral feedback to working sessions with the senior vice president and by November were able to make recommendations. They decided to concentrate upon those ABMS dealing with regular agents rather than special agents. The ABM would now be called a manager. He was to spend one third of his time in the office dealing with agents and reviewing their performance with them; this would be based upon specified pre-work by each. Communication was to be two-way, with the manager explaining policy and receiving intelligence. Agents were also to take part in weekly group meetings in the developing of the branch marketing plan. In all this the managers were to be involved more in the information flow and in planning and would be initiators. They would still spend a high proportion of their time in the field, but their attitude would be expected to be managerial rather than selling.

The consultants focused upon the structural variable, proposing detailed changes in authority at head office, the region, and in the branch. The branch managers' new role was to manage the new managers (i.e. the former ABMS) rather than the agents as before. The changes in the content of the new managers' role was also reflected by changes in the reward system and the replacement of the sales trophy. The change plan was given a title, the Line Management System, and it was to be piloted by the consultants in three test branches, then by six senior executives in the next six branches, then by the regional managers. The change was to be total, not gradual, with no special off-the-job training scheme. Instead, there was an orientation period of four days during which the regional managers would discuss the specially prepared guides.

O'Connell observes, from his research on the period following the changeover, that the consultants' proposals had led to considerable changes in the behaviour of the target population, although there were deviations. They had begun to behave more like decentralized line managers.

4.3 Technological change in shipping (G. Hjelholt)

The study by Hjelholt is set in the Danish shipping industry where, in 1962, it had been planned that the introduction of highly automated tankers would be accompanied by a dramatic reduction in the over-all size of the crew and a consequent impact on both the pre-existing social structure of the ship as well as upon the 'rules of the game' governing relations between seafarers and the owners. Hjelholt, a social psychologist, describes how he assisted one crew in the anticipation of many of the social and organizational problems arising. His main strategies were use of conferences and role playing, with the personal performance of the behavioural scientist playing an important, though unobtrusive, part in creating the change.

Shipping represents another interesting area for the behavioural scientist. Although there have been few studies of seafaring communities (e.g. Barnes, 1954) and the social structure of ships (e.g. Aubert and Arner, 1958), there is considerable interest in the almost military character of organizing. Two features are relevant. First, there is the theme of crisis and survival. Second, there is the very hierarchical structure in which traditionally the captain has occupied a position of considerable importance and influence. Richardson, in a comparative study, shows that the prime focus of loyalty for crews on British ships is 'the company' and for American ships, 'the union'. His study also reveals that an 'intricate set of checks and counterchecks are continuously in play between mate, bosun and deck crowd'. It is into such a context, with its complex ramifications of onshore community life (e.g. Horobin, 1957), that technological change is being introduced. The general trend is towards increasing automation and an increasing rate of technological innovation in general. These, coupled with the reduced turn-around time in port and the extended time at sea for large tankers, are radically affecting life aboard ships. The repertoire of jokes, once central to the seafarers life, is seriously threatened by these developments, with consequent problems for interpersonal tension. Social and behavioural scientists have been increasingly associated with important studies of the implications of technological change (e.g. Thorsrud, 1970; Herbst, 1962). In this study we shall examine the instance in which Hjelholt was involved in preparing a crew for their transfer from a traditional tanker to one of the technically most automated tankers.

Shipping poses a number of special problems for the practitioner. An important area concerns the extent to which decisions should be made on board the ship or on shore. This problem is intimately connected to decisions about continuous versus temporary crewing. The decisions about these influence the allocation of tasks to roles and hence the fabric of the social structure. Any decisions made need to account for the simple fact of a decrease in the size of the crew, and some possibility of the fragmentation of the social system arising from the isolation of members and reduced opportunities for interaction with colleagues. Associated with this is the idealization of the previous system, disenchantment with the new role for the seafarer, and the breakup of seafaring communities. On board there is the difficulty of defining the 'rules of the game' governing work, non-work and private time. There are some grounds for being optimistic in that the application of sociotechnical design may bring about less hierarchical forms of organization that would provide opportunities for individual and social projects. In certain respects the transformation of the technology of shipping has the same kinds of implication for the self-image of the seafarer as does advanced weapons technology for the image of the military man (Abrams, 1962; Janowitz, 1959, 1964).

The context of Hjelholt's (1963) work in Denmark was the general increase in competition between shipping firms in the 1960s. Developments in the design of ships, particularly in automation, presented the opportunity for reducing the size of crews with the consequent possibility of being more competitive. This was only possible if the crews and their union organization were prepared to accept reduced manning, changed job content, and changed relations of status and influence within the crew. One of Denmark's most technologically progressive companies gained permission from the government to introduce an experiment for one year with a reduced crew on an automated tanker which was being commissioned. Relations between the owners and the unions were characterized by periods of intense conflict, and this particular experiment was opposed by the unions.

Hjelholt was given a free hand in devising the training. The account he gives of this does contain some suggestion that the shipping owners viewed the training as a special opportunity to pass on information to the selected crew and felt that the social psychologist could provide expert advice in achieving this. In contrast, Hjelholt places more emphasis upon the 'building' of the new role system.

It was expected that the tanker would be ready in December, 1962. Hjelholt planned:

- a five-day conference in September
- technical training of the crew
- a second conference in mid-November

Eight representatives of the new crew and several participants from the company offices attended the first conference in September. On the first day, experts from the head office presented technical details, and neither Hjelholt nor his assistant attempted to take leadership. On the next day, when the group was alone, Hjelholt undertook a more initiatory posture. He defined the aims of the conference as taking decisions that would fulfil the needs of those who would work on board the new tanker. The main restriction was that any decisions should be within company policy and that all decisions should be unanimous. If a unanimous decision could not be achieved, the captain alone would decide. The role of the company experts was defined as advisory, and any further decisions had to be acceptable to the deckhands, who were not represented at the first conference.

The group then listed the areas in which they wanted to plan. These included meal arrangements, alcohol regulations, location of quarters, use of leisure, safety and maintenance. Discussion of these topics began in an atmosphere of general anxiety, particularly amongst the representatives from the engine room. The members of the conference were allocated to small groups to discuss different topics (e.g. the role of the deck crew), and Hjelholt's role was to carry out an analysis of the 'group process'. The groups reported to Hjelholt that they found great difficulty in planning for the unknown.

On the fourth day Hjelholt chaired a meeting of the whole group. He describes the group process as one of 'fight-flight' (Bion, 1951). That is to say, when a member undertook a leadership role he was subject to attack until he abdicated and the whole process was repeated. On the final day, summaries were made in preparation for the later meeting. Suddenly the group began to discuss the problem of how they could feel responsible. In their evaluation of the first conference, the members expressed the feeling that the exercise had been worthwhile.

At the November meeting, three additional members of the crew were present. Again the meeting began slowly and Hjelholt commented that morale was low. By the third day tensions had built up and were directed against a visitor from the company offices. The last two days were more successful. The conference made a relatively radical proposal, namely, that weekly planning meetings should be held on the new tanker. On the final day the ship's captain was in the chair and the conference made some thirteen decisions. This development reflects an agreement of decision making by consensus. With the taking of responsibility, the group began to conduct the 'process analysis', and the captain took on the position of 'managing director'. It was decided that the reports to the Danish Ministry of Shipping and Commerce should include the observations of the various groups on the new tanker.

The new tanker was commissioned and in service by mid-December. In February, Hjelholt travelled with the crew from Japan to the Persian Gulf. He carried out observations in all parts of the tanker, using his special role to articulate tensions between sections and to ensure that the job enlargement which the changes in manning required were being carried through.

An inspection of the tanker some twelve months after the start of the experiment showed that maintenance had been at a very high level; that overtime had been greatly reduced; that there had been only one disciplinary case; and that the crew was largely satisfied with the tanker. When the reports of the success of the experiment were circulated, there was some hostility and opposition to the innovation, but the crew was not deterred. Hjelholt attributed the success to 'participative planning'.

4.4   Organizational design for a new factory (P. A. Clark)

In 1967 a specially appointed assessment committee within a well-known British manufacturer in the consumer industry decided to replace its existing production facilities of three semi-autonomous factories by one new integrated factory which would be technologically the most advanced of its kind in the world and would incorporate the company's new concept of employee relations and participation. We shall give the firm the pseudonym of CCE Ltd and the location of its plant, marketing, and research and development facilities, Provincial City. The nine-man specially constituted top-level group, given the task of guiding and implementing the new concept, we shall call the Azimuth Group (see Clark and Cherns, 1970; P. A. Clark, 1972).

In mid-1967, after making a broad sweep of main requirements, the Azimuth Group had a preliminary sketch of what the new factory would need to contain in the way of equipment. They also had estimates of proposed manning at all levels. At this stage, key members of Azimuth began to explore the motivational problems raised by the new technology and through a chain of events came into contact with our university-based centre specializing in research and development in the social sciences. They invited A. B. Cherns, Professor of Social Sciences, who had considerable experience in applied research in the military and was intimately concerned with applications, and myself to discuss the problems. We heard about their proposals, toured the plant to see existing equipment, and returned to the conference room to make suggestions to members of Azimuth. Cherns emphasized that we could play a role but the nature of the relationship had to be a dialogue, that is, joint agreement on priorities and some joint pieces of investigation. The chairman agreed, but then told us he heard that on our tour we had made some critical comments about the sketch designs for the layout and organization of the plant. From this chance set of comments began the focus upon organizational design for a new factory at a green fields site.

Organizational design is concerned with the means utilized to handle the management and coordination of an enterprise and is distinguished from job design by the requirement for dealing with the organization as a whole in relation to its external environment. Katz and Kahn contend, rightly, that the design of future organizational behaviour should be part of forward planning in all enterprises. There are few examples, but exponents of the sociotechnical approach* and the contingency theories provide valuable and complementary perspectives tackling the task, technical, and structure variables from the Leavitt scheme. I would argue that there is an important neglect of the people variable, and in the project at CCE we tackled this by undertaking studies to determine the actual orientations of employees. The sociotechnical approach has been used extensively by members of the Tavistock Institute of Human Relations; by Thorsrud and Herbst from the Oslo Work Research Institute; and by L. E. Davis and J. Taylor at the Graduate School for Organizational Studies, UCLA.

The first diagnostic phase, which I myself conducted for some three months, was directed at gaining an understanding of the ways in which the firm was organized, its recent history, and its immediate plans. This included an examination of CCE as an open system emphasizing the marketing aspect and the means used to coordinate for product innovations. The diagnosis concerned Azimuth, but their anxieties were in part allayed by the prompt manner in which Cherns tackled a specific question they had about the provision of amenities. From the diagnosis it was apparent that there were a number of tensions in the proposed plans. First, there were signs that the composition of the market would fragment for some products with a consequent effect for production scheduling and batch sizes that did not obviously fit the proposals for the new technology. Second, the changed nature of interdependencies between departments became crucial because the total throughput time fell from one hundred hours to less than ten, and the time balance between two major departments was a matter of minutes rather than hours. This obviously had considerable implications for the control system. Third, the analysis of the proposed technology indicated that decision making would be taking place at higher levels in the management, whilst it was the aim of Azimuth to retain the existing pattern of delegated decision making.

The question arose of how to make some of these important points relevant. To do this we undertook a specific study of one major department that would be directly affected by the proposed technology. We were able to show that the existing form of organization was one in

---

* The sociotechnical approach is a broad analytic scheme usually, but not necessarily, allied with the choice of autonomous groups as favoured solution. For a critical view of the solution and development of the analysis see E. Miller and A. K. Rice, 1967, and my own usage in P. A. Clark, 1972.

which interdependent tasks had for historical reasons been delegated to independent groups of operators who manned the machines. The form of organization approximated to what Trist would call the autonomous group, and thus represented the form of organizing that many firms are seeking to implement. Yet, ironically, the plans of the R & D team would lead to the removal of this aspect. In this way we were able to establish a data base for convincing Azimuth that there were very significant *differences* between existing and future plant. Feedback occurred both informally and through two main meetings which were stormy and controversial, but at which we were adamant about the relevance of the findings. Fortunately, our approach had included the building in of the capability for using the results in the design of the study. We had undertaken the investigation within a modified sociotechnical approach (see Clark, 1972, chap. 7) in joint partnership with R & D, work study, and other functions. Also, our team had been strengthened by the addition of a technologist and, for a period, by another sociologist. Although controversial and in part puzzling the project continued, but we had learnt the relevance of clarifying our activities, and therefore decided to focus on the creation of *alternative* sociotechnical design.

In this phase of the project we selected a fairly simple part of the technology to pilot a form of scenario writing in short-life project groups composed of external social scientists and internal designers and affected parties. This phase moved fairly smoothly, and although there was no firm agreement on the solution selected from the alternatives, the strategy of joint working was felt sufficiently viable to apply to major and key departments. Thus a new group was established following the same principles of gradually reconstructing the social structure and organization implied by existing plans, and generating alternatives which optimized both the social and technical systems. However, the new group experienced considerable difficulties in proceeding and was reconstituted on several occasions. I would suggest that the explanation for this lies in both the complexity of analysis and the difficulty which some had in taking into account the ways in which decisions had to be made when a number of factors were unknown. The study showed quite clearly that the concept of the technical system was subject to continual modification, and sometimes to total shift as new evidence emerged of changing market conditions. In making the selection amongst several alternative sociotechnical designs, it was necessary to undertake a careful examination of the social structure and to balance this by an operational research analysis of the work flow by one member of our team.

In this later phase, running into the third year of the project, we undertook studies of the social relations and values of both production and maintenance workers as well as investigating the management organization by examining the pattern of authority and interaction through the use of Scott's Diagram (see E. L. Scott, 1956). The focus was upon identifying the prevailing subculture – especially the differences between groups – and locating preferences about modes of organizing. We considered that organizational design should include data on the preferences of those involved.

In addition to the particular decisions reached, the members of the Azimuth Group reported that the joint study had focused their attention upon the actual behaviour and expectations of employees and that the approach had been positive.

I had attempted to formalize some aspects by isolating the emphasis upon *differences* between the planned and the actual, and combining this with the generation of *alternatives*, to create ADA, the Alternatives and Differences Approach to organizational design. We had hoped to follow the pattern set by Whyte and Hamilton (1964) by institutionalizing the behavioural science input, but internal developments somewhat nipped that hope in the bud.

One general point: the dialogue proposed by Cherns involved considerable conflict and confrontation. It is more than likely that the willingness of Azimuth to accept and work with this in the spirit of enquiry so central to action research was facilitated by their exposure to the first phase of the Managerial Grid. Our role was gradually routinized throughout the four and a half years of the project in the manner posited by Jones.

4.5 Accident rates and morale in the military (T. T. Paterson)

The occurrence of several major wars in the past 60 years has had a formative influence upon the extent and form of use made of the behavioural sciences in North America and Europe.

In World War I the Americans and the British made considerable use of psychological testing, employing experts in full-time work on placement and training. After the end of hostilities this situation

E

changed somewhat dramatically, though there is good reason for arguing that the content and focus of academic psychology had been significantly influenced. The role of the military psychologists became more strongly established after 1945 though there has been a tendency, according to Lang, for their activities to have become largely routinized. In World War II, these social psychologists, especially in the United States (Stouffer *et al.*, 1949), became involved in studies of the factors influencing the morale of soldiers and civilians with regard to the opposing armies of the time. This work, with its focus upon the small group as a key unit of analysis, influenced post-war thinking in the behavioural sciences and industry. After the war, the American military gave very considerable support to research. This was largely of the basic objective type, and included studies of leadership and morale undertaken in a variety of university departments. The Office of Naval Research supported a great deal of work significant to the development of the behavioural sciences. They also influenced the mode of dissemination.

The military represents a special kind of user of behavioural science, and we may anticipate that the strategies of action research developed in industrial contexts would not necessarily be transferable, even within the same society. J. A. A. van Doorn has shown with reference to the European scene that the emergence of the officer corps as an entity in which the profession and the organization were fused was a long and complex process of transferring aristocratically based images into the context of the most technologically sophisticated enterprise in modern society. Janowitz, in a penetrating portrait of this transformation from different origins in the United States – the internal wars – to the concept of 'armed peace', highlights the problems of adjustment. The relevance of the military is that its complexity of primary tasks, with their ever changing priorities, is complicated further by a range of secondary tasks. In handling these there is considerable emphasis upon sustaining internal co-ordination, and it is perhaps this feature of the code of rules governing relations between the members of the officer corps (i.e. the military subculture) which is most likely to hinder overt action research. This may explain the tactics adopted by Paterson in the case study we present now.

In 1941 Paterson was sent to an airfield in the southwest of England. He was a ground officer. On arrival he found that his first major assignment was to tackle the recently increased accident rate amongst pilots. The main activities were patrols of shipping lanes, observation of convoys, weather reconnaissance, mining, and occasional rare contact with the enemy.

The high accident rate was blamed upon the state of the runways. Paterson's first response was almost classical: he attempted to establish an association between scores on reaction-time tests and involvement in accidents. No association was discovered. Second, he attempted to introduce further flying training, but Paterson found that this was not taken seriously. Through his close personal contact and observation of many groups on the airfield, he began to discern some major patterns of association, conflict, and cleavage. These observations became expecially important when he discovered from analysis of the accident statistics that the increase had been largely associated with the arrival of squadrons from an airfield which had good runways.

Paterson drew upon his analysis of 'mess politics', particularly the lack of confidence between the 'flying crews' and 'ground types', to interpret the blaming of the runways as a rationalization of a more complex problem. He hypothesized that the causes of accidents were social, not physical or technical. In his analysis he argues that the fliers were a high status group, who because of their performance in the Battle of Britain were generally accorded high prestige by other groups on the airfield. In this instance the fliers were not accorded the high prestige they expected because the ground types felt that the non-combat nature of the tasks did not warrant it. Thus the absence of direct combat becomes crucial in understanding the individual and collective frustration of the fliers. The consequence of this frustration is aggression and hostility within the flying crews and between them and other groups. Paterson's observations suggested to him three lines for action:

1. The creation of an alternative symbolic enemy to externalize aggression.
2. The improvement of morale within the flying groups.
3. The improvement of morale between the flying groups and the rest of the airfield.

At this stage he explained part of his interpretation to the Commanding Officer, who attempted to tackle the situation through the obvious channel of a pep talk. Paterson then began to search for a means of intervention that would take account of the need for a symbolic enemy. He decided that the weather would form a suitable alternative focus, especially because the airfield was located in an area subject to highly changeable conditions which introduced certain hazards. The major problem was one of disseminating and gaining the adoption of his new focus. He decided that the success of this dissemination process was dependent upon an analysis of the patterns of influence and power among the various groups. In practice it was necessary to develop a typology of informal social roles and a theory that would explain their part in the influence process. The typology and theory, later known as the *methetic* theory of group relations, trichotomized group roles in terms of influence:

1. The OUT-GROUP contains two roles:
   Social isolate. Physically part of the collectivity, but excluded from influence upon values and actions.
   Eccentric. Allowed a very circumscribed influence upon the group.
2. The IN-GROUP contains three roles:
   Exemplar. Represents the central values of the dominant coalition within the group. Typically non-vociferous in the English culture.
   Exdominus. A spokesman and leader in group action, but dependent upon the statement of a 'norm' by the occupants of examplar roles. The role is concerned with external relations.
   Indominus. Concerned with relations within the group and enforces conformity. Exercises social control and plays a significant part in holding the group together. Handles deviance by joking and encouragement.
3. The MIMETIC role is that of the follower, and it is most associated in Paterson's analysis with the in-group roles.

(However, it may be noted in terms of the process approach to analysis advocated in Section 9.1 that this definition is too restricted.)

The methetic theory states that group action is dependent upon the statement of the norm* or ideal to be followed. The person associated with crystallizing this norm for the group is termed the exemplar. Once the norm is defined, the exdominus can relate the norm to action and the indominus can attempt to ensure conformity to the ideal and the action. Paterson constructed the typology in order to identify the various persons in the key groups who could play a part in the dis-

---

* This theory of group norms does tend to underplay the availability of counter values; it may be a reflection of the military subculture to which it was applied.

semination of focus on his proposed symbolic enemy. He aimed to work with the exemplars initially and then, once the idea was introduced, move on to the exdominus and indominus role-takers in order to establish constructive plans that would crystallize the focus upon the weather. Paterson describes in some detail how he undertook this, and argues that its success is demonstrated by a dramatic fall in the accident rate.

As a case study, Paterson's is one of the most detailed and informative about the practitioner's conception of the problem, the theory applied to the problem, and the means of intervention adopted. As such it has a practical and theoretical relevance which has so far been neglected. A critique of the account might well suggest that other factors were influential, but that is not within the immediate concern of this chapter.

4.6 Job enrichment in the process industry (W. Paul, F. Herzberg and K. B. Robertson)

The design of jobs has been increasingly delegated to experts from industrial engineering, work study, and allied disciplines. Job design has become in part an unintended consequence of the plans of engineers and accountants for the most efficient operation of the technical system. Thus, such factors as batch size can affect the organization of work and the opportunities for satisfactory working environments. Work study and production engineering increased rapidly after 1945 and became the owners of job design. Then its philosophy was criticized by social scientists (e.g. Friedmann, 1955, 1961), and a very considerable body of research was undertaken to demonstrate that its underlying theories about human motivation were inadequate.

In response to the challenge from industrial engineers for alternative theories of job design, the psychologists frequently suggested job rotation and job enlargement. However, both of these largely accept the existing situation and seek to ameliorate it. The breakthrough in thinking about motivation and job design came after the publication of the researches of F. Herzberg and colleagues. They adopted what has been regarded as a somewhat unusual approach to the study of motivation. They asked a sample of two hundred accountants and engineers in the United States to recall periods in their past five years at work when they felt particularly good or bad about their jobs. From this, the researchers collected some 480 incidents. Additionally,

the respondents were asked to report whether the feelings of pleasure
or disgruntlement lasted for a short or a long time. The date were
analysed under fourteen major headings. The extended analysis of
these revealed important distinctions between factors that were a
source of satisfaction or dissatisfaction (hygiene factors) and those
that were a source of motivation. This led the researchers to postulate
the two-factor theory, which asserts that factors concerned with the
context of a job – supervision, working conditions, salary, relations
with colleagues – are essentially a source of satisfaction rather than
motivation. The interesting feature of the theory is that it is just these
contextual factors which have the source focus of the major thrust in
personnel policies during the past two decades, yet they are at best
the source of satisfaction rather than motivation. In contrast, the
content of the job is found to be crucial as a source of potential motivation. Content refers to the extent to which the job offers opportunities
for personal growth, for advancement and recognition. It is just this
area which has, ironically, been delegated to the systems expert and
industrial engineer. Though this formulation appears somewhat simple,
it is in fact revolutionary when compared with the existing ideas about
motivation.

The work of Herzberg and colleagues became gradually better
known during the 1960s, especially through major journals such as
the *Harvard Business Review* and through management training courses.
Potential users became aware of the theory and some were interested
in considering its application to the design of jobs. In this chapter we
are not directly concerned with the controversy which has surrounded
the theory. Critics have attacked almost every aspect of the researches,
but they do not appear to have radically influenced the acceptability
of the ideas to managers. It should be noted that Herzberg was not
concerned with people's opinions about a given work situation, but
with their experiences of different work situation. He was not concerned
with the differences between individuals and cultures, but with different
kinds of events (Paul and Robertson, 1970). It is argued that different
events have a different psychological dynamic, and tend to produce
special kinds of response in people, irrespective of the individual or
group culture.

The findings were supported in other contexts (Myers, 1965) and
the theory of 'hygiene factors' and 'motivators' became part of the
stock of knowledge that teachers presented to students and to experi-

enced managers. Initially there was no instrumented programme comparable to the technology of work study for implementing the philosophy. In Britain the Imperial Chemical Industries, who had been leaders in the application of work study, now began to play a crucial role in the application of behavioural science.

Throughout the 1960s Imperial Chemical Industries (ICI) had taken a careful and critical outlook toward the social and behavioural sciences.

The form and content of the experiment have considerable implications for action research and the application of the behavioural sciences. It is already apparent that the success has influenced traditional thinking in the UK about job design. Indeed one senior executive who had been a pacemaker in disseminating the philosophy and approach of Job Enrichment recently commented that the dissemination had almost been too successful.

The ICI example is of interest because it illustrates the influence, both direct and indirect, that a major enterprise can have on the establishment of new industrial specialisms. In the 1950s ICI had been strongly associated with the introduction of work study, and members of that company had played a leading role in the professionalization of work study in the UK and in Europe. Similarly, many members have recently been active in disseminating the findings of the more recent experiments in job design. Given that job design projects only formed a small proportion of the behavioural science projects in the sample of American industry conducted by Rush, it may be seen that the legitimation of behavioural science by a major and distinguished firm can strongly influence the extent and pace at which the traditional territory of psychologists is expanded.

4.7 Mergers and market changes at Sigma (L. B. Barnes and L. E. Greiner)

This case study examines the application of the Managerial Grid (see Section 3.4) at the Sigma plant (pseudonym). The research on it was undertaken by members of one of the key contributors to the examination of organizational change.

Sigma was part of a larger petro-chemical company, 'Piedmont', which was merged in 1960. This merger changed Sigma's relationship with its head office and occurred at a time when a twenty-five-year contract based on cost plus profit was terminated. The head office was particularly concerned about the way in which manpower was being used to carry out construction work and felt that the plan was over-manned. Within Sigma there were strong strains between different departments and levels, dysfunctional to the smooth running of the complex technology which required constant interdepartment cooperation. Mistakes were costly and sometimes dangerous. The plant manager, formerly a highly regarded technical executive, tried to identify the problems but found difficulty in gaining acceptance. This problem was exacerbated by union activity. Although the plant invested heavily in training programmes for its eight hundred managers and supervisers, the management had not discovered a way of relating the concerns for people to those for production. The plant had developed a rigid and polarized management system to cope with this environment, but the system seemed inadequate in the face of new demands that arose after 1958, when the product market became more competitive and turbulent.

In the context of an uncertain environment and a worsening relationship between the local management at Sigma and the headquarters some distance away, the performance and morale of the plant deteriorated. Blake entered in 1961 at the suggestion of the headquarters, and though Sigma management felt that Blake was a competent man they did not consider that he could help with their specific problems. Blake began a diagnosis, including the use of off-site laboratories, to obtain a degree of confrontation between the management at Sigma and headquarters. Relations between the two improved, the pressure on Sigma was reduced, and the local management then began to concentrate upon the internal problems at the plant, using a variety of approaches including the Managerial Grid.

The first phase of the organizational development programme, designed to remove the internal blockages and create more constructive and creative conflicts, began in November 1962 when forty managers attended a one-week Managerial Grid seminar. By mid-1963 more than eight hundred managers and technical men had participated, and the earlier participants commenced the later phases. In significant respects the programme was run by line managers with staff experts and consultants playing peripheral roles.

This application raises a number of questions: Can the programme assist in translating behavioural science concepts into action? Can it achieve significant attitudinal changes without dysfunctional consequences for individuals? Can management take primary responsibility? Barnes and Greiner sought to answer these and other questions by looking at the consequences of the programme, especially the concomitant changes in productivity, in practices and behaviour, and in perceptions. They are the first to emphasize the difficulty of this task, and are clearly aware of the limitations of a simplistic evaluation or assumption that changes in profitability are directly associated with the Managerial Grid. In this sense they have an excellent awareness of the haloing tendency in accounts of the uses of the behavioural sciences (see Clark and Ford, 1970).

First, with respect to productivity Barnes and Greiner note almost dramatic improvements in performace during and after the programme; they caution that many factors are uncontrollable and therefore they isolated the improvements in manpower utilization which are attributable to improved operating procedures and higher productivity. These improvements were responsible for savings amounting to several million dollars. Further, it is suggested that the Grid facilitated a better development of group solutions amongst managers in a way that directly increased profits. In general, members attending the Grid reported a significant increase in the extent and quality of decisions. This facet is said also to be evidenced in the kinds of follow-up project initiated in the final phase of the Grid programme.

Second, it is reported that there were changes in practices and behaviour. For example, the frequency of group meetings increased, especially amongst administrative managers. There was a change in the criteria used to assess performance and promotion, and an increase in the amount of internal transferability of personnel about the plant.

Thirdly, there were changes in attitude, especially with respect to change in the rules of the game governing intergroup and interdepartmental relationships. This was evident in the shift from thinking characterized by 'either-or' and 'compromise' to an integrative synthesis. It is suggested that the changes were rapid and previously polarized attitudes reversed.

CHAPTER 5

The uneasy partnership

In the natural sciences a complex network exists that links and separates the research, teaching, and practitioner systems. In the behavioural sciences, the division of labour is less well defined and there is no convincing argument that suggests that the growth and institutionalization of behavioural science will follow a similar pattern (see Lippitt, 1965; Jenkins and Velody, 1969). All that we can expect is a reduction in the influence of the universities and a growth in the number of persons and professions associated with the creation and application of the behavioural sciences within organizations.

In this chapter we briefly examine the more commonly used categories applied to persons who are associated with planned organizational change. We shall be most concerned with developing a terminology to aid understanding.

We start with two neglected facts. First, there are considerable differences between the kinds of roles adopted by behavioural scientists and so a range of titles has emerged: consultant, researcher, trainer, designer. Second, there are various distinct and overlapping roles played by the members of sponsoring enterprises, yet there has been a tendency to regard sponsors as homogeneous when in fact they are highly differentiated. (It follows that we should expect action research to have both supporters and opponents within any sponsoring system.)

5.1 Sponsors

A feature of action research and organizational change is that we know remarkably little about the role of the sponsor. We may define sponsors as the persons who both sanction and allocate resources, time and money for the undertaking of assignments involving either behavioural scientists or elements of behavioural science in the form of a package. It is generally agreed that the role of the sponsor is significant, if not crucial, because of the non-routinized nature of action research programmes. Sponsors may or may not be the subjects for organizational change. For example, the sponsors of Hjelholt's work (Section 4.3) employed an outside consultant in order to facilitate the changing of practices and attitudes of a subject population, the crew of the new tanker. The sponsors of the job enrichment study (Section 4.6) were similarly motivated. In contrast, much of organizational development directly involves the sponsor, at least in the early stages, and is built upon the notion of total change at all levels. My study at CCE (4.4) suggests that the sponsors were indirectly subjects but that much of the work was undertaken in studies of orientations of sections of the work force who were to move to the new factory. It is convenient to separate sponsors and subjects, and important to do so in order to understand action research, because some subject populations are active in relation to action research whilst others are not (see Section 9.1). On one project I was working on in the military, the nature of sponsorship changed at varying levels and differing stages of project. An important factor in inhibiting the developments of the project was that we had not successfully managed to relate to a variety of influential subject populations. The distinction between sponsors and subjects points to the importance of the sanctioning of organizational change (see Jaques, 1951).

Jones gives careful attention to the role of the intelligent layman within sponsoring enterprises. Though the distinction he makes is simple, it is useful and provides the possibility of development when linked to the models of organizational change. Jones principally emphasizes the *change catalyst* and the *pacemaker*. The catalyst speeds up and slows down the change process. He is most active in the early stages of a project and is not necessarily involved in every stage. The catalyst cannot alter the general focus, but can facilitate or inhibit. Catalysts are unlikely to be behavioural scientists and their style is characterized by paternalism. Their influence in the sponsoring system is subtle and pervasive and complicates the relationship between the practitioner and the sponsoring system, particularly because the catalyst constantly switches power positions to influence the change.

The pacemaker concept draws heavily on the analogy of medical technology. The pacemaker is an agent or agents who are exogenous to the part of the system that is the target of change. His role is to ensure that the predetermined and newly established level of performance is maintained. Hence he does not introduce change, but guarantees its maintenance. Jones concedes that the pacemaker concept is based upon conjecture and that the connection between his discussion of the role, based as it is on analogies with control engineering and the data he is attempting to order in terms of the concept, is tenuous.

Another role found in many action research projects, is that of the appointed *linkman*. The sponsor, or sponsoring group, is rarely involved in the week-to-week running of the project or the interpretation of its activities to other members of the enterprise. This role is usually allocated to a person we may call the linkman. He is usually full-time, or largely so, and plays a crucial role. For example, in the CCE Ltd project (Section 4.4), the linkman at one stage was an experienced industrial relations negotiator who applied his skill and insight to establishing the principle of scenario writing with one of the short-life project groups. His performance in matching the idea to the potential in the situation was crucial.

Finally we may note that within the sponsoring organization those who oppose action research are frequently described as resistant to change and their role is presented by some practitioners as destructive. Two comments are relevant. First, opponents of change, just as promoters, may have a variety of good motives. Second, some commentators have observed that there is an aspect which is actually functional to the success of the project – this point is implicit in Klein's analysis of the defender's role (Klein, 1969).

5.2   Practitioners

Practitioners may be located within the sponsoring system (as in the increasing number of in-house behavioural science sections and departments), in research agencies and institutes, in specialized consultancies, or in the academic system. Generally observers have distinguished between the positions of those located within the sponsoring system and those outside. The theoretical justification for this is not clear, and the claims that one is more effective would not seem to be supported by the evidence presented. Given that in part the internal-external distinction is based on beliefs about relative influence, it is worth noting Jones's observation, drawn from a content analysis of some two hundred cases, to the effect that there is a marginal, though not significant, balance in favour of the external agent. However, we must note that there is a general lack of empirical work. The recent researches on the uses of behavioural science in the industrial, urban, and welfare areas of Holland by Mark van de Vall* contain questions on this topic taken across 120 carefully sampled cases. It seems likely that the publication of his analysis will clarify the issue.

Frequently the term 'change agent' has been applied to practitioners, especially by Rogers (1961) in his study of the diffusion of practices (Section 12.2), and by Bennis. The advantages of this term are not obvious. As we have seen from the interacting-variable schema of Leavitt, it is possible for change to arise from a variety of sources and to be planned or unplanned. Our case studies include an example of a management consultant achieving change. Teachers might justifiably claim to be change agents, and so on, and so on. It seems preferable to examine whether these people do achieve change, and to ascertain its nature and direction, before allowing the name to obscure the reality. However, we should not ignore the ideological implications of the term. I shall prefer to speak of practitioners.

The term 'practitioner' covers an increasing number of separate specialisms which can be disaggregated for the purposes of under-standing and analysis. Before doing so, we must consider one general point of relevance. There has been an assumption in academically based research that the role of the scientist outside the university is fraught with tensions and dissatisfactions because it is not isomorphic with that of the academic researcher. I would want to argue that the assumption should be a hypothesis, and as such we already have sound circum-stantial evidence for rejecting it. The evidence arises from two locations: first, we know from the increasing number of researches on schools, colleges, and universities that only part of the student popula-tion is oriented to academic goals; second, we know from studies conducted on scientists in industry that they do not necessarily experience role strain or conflict because of a preference for the academic role. They may experience bewilderment at the disparity between the academic's model of research outside universities and the reality, but that is another matter. For convenience it is useful to think of the practitioner as part of a set of actors who are oriented to solution of practical problems, who are essentially organizational scientists rather than academic scientists. However, we should not press the point too far.

* Mark van de Vall, Department of Sociology, Buffalo University, undertook the research in the Netherlands in 1970–1971 and is concerned in directing the analysis.

The wide variety of new roles for practitioners includes researchers, trainers, teachers, counsellors and development designers. Given that there are both research agencies and in-house sections, we may expect this increasing division of labour, although it is apparent from the case studies in Chapter 4 that many roles may be played by the same person in the process of completing one organizational change programme. *Researchers* refers to those engaged in activities identified by the predominance of a concern with techniques of data collection and analysis, as in feedback analysis (see Heller, 1970). *Trainers* typically refers to specialists in sensitivity training and in organizational development. *Teachers* is applied to those specializing in human relations programmes. *Counsellors* may be taken to include those specializing in dealing with individual employee problems of the kinds identified by those associated with the Hawthorne experiments in Chicago in the 1920s. *Development designers* are concerned with a new set of tasks; as Bowers (1970) envisages this role it is primarily involved in relating developments in research areas to ongoing professional practice and is especially fruitful in the creation of instrumented technologies and their modification (see Section 12.3).

The situation for the practitioner is just as Bennis suggests. The final shape of the practitioner's role is not yet clear, and it is hazardous to describe exactly what practitioners do on the basis of their reports. Similar comments are made by Trist when overviewing difficulties in decoding how even the best-known practitioners proceed, even when one is able to observe them in action.

The way the role is occupied and defined will depend significantly, though not entirely, on the ambitions and competences of the increasing numbers of graduates from the behavioural sciences who are entering, either directly or indirectly, into the practitioner role. They have been described by Trist as a third force which will significantly influence the extent and opportunity for action research.

The case studies in Chapter 4 illustrated the variety of roles that practitioners actually take. For example, the research role is strong in the CCE study and the development design role is implicit in the work of Paul and colleagues on job enrichment. It is clear that practitioners have to be both flexible and adaptable.

CHAPTER 6

Valid knowledge

Practitioners have tended to use the term 'valid knowledge' to describe the three main characteristics of the perspectives they adopt. In this chapter we shall examine the concept of valid knowledge, pointing to the important ways in which it differs from the kinds of explanation and understanding required by scientists. These differences will be presented in the form of an exaggerated typification. However, these contrasts should not be allowed to obscure the role of theory in action research, particularly of one type which we term goal-based empirical theory.

6.1 Focus introduced

The practitioner utilizes three main kinds of knowledge in his diagnosis and solution of the sponsor's problem and situation. First, there are the concepts, variables, and propositions both from the basic disciplines of the behavioural sciences and from interdisciplinary approaches. We have emphasized earlier (see Section 3.1) that it is these items, forming as they do the perspective and subject matter of the study of organizational change, which are the distinguishing features of the behavioural science practitioner's approach. We would expect, and we find, that management scientists in operational research select a quite different set of concepts, variables, and propositions (see Bennis, 1969, pp. 65–66). The behavioural scientist's selection should allow him to make an analysis of the sponsoring enterprise in a manner that takes account of internal processes and functioning within the context of the external environment. The propositions utilized should be those that search for key interdependencies between external factors (such as the kinds of market competition) and the degree of separation of functional areas within the enterprise. It thus should allow the practitioner to examine the behaviour of members as it actually exists at the time of the change programme and should be able to account for the critical events and factors which brought about the existing situation. Additionally, it should be capable of allowing the practitioner to reconstruct how proposed changes to the existing situation will affect the key attributes.

67

Within this intellectual tool-kit the practitioner has a small number of items which we call social inventions (see Section 3.4). These are clearly formulated packages which can be used as solutions to certain specified problems. We have referred to the Managerial Grid, and to this we may add the autonomous group as utilized by many socio-technical analysts (see Sections 4.4; 9.3) and the participative form of management identified by Likert and known as System 4 (Likert, 1967). The main problem which these social inventions raise is that of deciding where they can be best applied. In practice, there are too few carefully documented studies of even the most frequently used inventions (see Section 12.3).

Second, from within the broader perspective of concepts, variables and propositions, the practitioner will make a further selection of key variables to identify the points in the system that he believes he can most successfully manipulate to achieve organizational change. The practitioner should attempt to choose variables that are important, that directly affect the target situation, and that are open to manipulation (see O'Connell, 1968, pp. 55–56). This selection will therefore include propositions that focus upon the dynamics of change and are open to empirical proof and refutation. Also included will be variables which the policy maker and decision taker can understand, manipulate and evaluate. This selection will reflect the specialist concerns of the practitioner, and will almost certainly incorporate his *beliefs* about the nature of man's role in society. We have already noted examples of this in the emphasis upon opening up bureaucracies as described by Bennis in his advocacy of organizational-development change strategies. Usually we can identify the essential features of an emphasis – where we can, we shall refer to it as the *focus* of the practitioner.

Thirdly, valid knowledge includes the particular data collected from the sponsoring system. We have seen from the case studies that this can involve an extensive and lengthy process of investigation, sometimes undertaken over several years. Thus Paterson (see Section 4.5) attempted to implement standard solutions without a diagnosis but soon noticed their failure; he switched to a thorough examination of observed behaviour for all groups, and also to the analysis of existing data such as accident reports. In our work at CCE (see Section 4.4) we used a wide variety of techniques including films, extensive interviews, observation and analysis of labour statistics to construct the required picture of the existing enterprise. We also had to analyse the drawings of engineers, the charts of work-study men, and the reports of the manpower studies, in order to identify where changes would take place.

The collection of information about the sponsoring enterprise may be undertaken in a variety of ways, but generally practitioners design their methods of collection to ensure that the end products will be seen as valid by the sponsor. Thus we note that the Managerial Grid obtains data on current performance and the assessment of excellence directly from those most intimately concerned. Similarly, Revans's approach concentrates upon the sponsor as the collector of information. This is obviously one aspect of both applied and action research which distinguishes them from basic research, and we shall examine this more extensively in the analysis of intervention strategies (Chapter 8).

The relevance of this threefold definition of valid knowledge is that it takes account of the unique features of the sponsoring system; that it facilitates the identification of the distinctive facets of the major problems to be solved; and that it draws in a discriminating fashion upon the basic disciplines. The selection should be guided by the requirements of the situation and the practitioner's judgements about relevance. Our definition gives strong support to the thorough diagnosis of the sponsoring system as suggested by Lawrence and Lorsch (1969).

Our definition of valid knowledge does not commit the practitioner to a particular type of solution; we still must confront the difficult task of determining how knowledge that may be largely research-based can be related to the specific circumstance of the sponsor. The question, does a theoretical principle hold for the sponsor's situation?, raises the problems of comparability between one situation and other research studies being considered (see Likert and Lippitt, 1953). Related to this problem is the difficulty of discerning 'what causes what' and deciding how it may guide 'what will happen if . . .'. In practice, action research requires a great deal of general and special information to understand the particular position of the sponsor. An important consideration for the practitioner is deciding whether to acquire a detailed knowledge himself or whether to establish linkages with persons who possess this knowledge. A great deal of time can be wasted by attempting to obtain knowledge that is readily available if the project team is expanded on a temporary basis by co-option.*

* See the strategy for data collection used in the early stages of the Managerial Grid. Also my use of short-life project groups in Section 4.4 and in Clark, 1972, chap. 6. See also Hutte, 1968.

F

The definition of valid knowledge reflects the emphasis given by the practitioner to elements that are not necessarily stressed in academic discourse. For example, the sponsor's role in sanctioning the knowledge as valid is central to its employment in an action research programme. Such evidence as we have indicates a low congruence between what sponsors and practitioners regard as good pieces of research. Dunnette and Brown (1968) attempted to assess the impact of sociological and psychological research on management. They asked industrial psychologists to rank a number of studies on the dimensions of predictive potential, verifiability, fruitfulness, and over-all value. Managers were asked to rank the same studies on the dimensions of 'heard of it', influenced behaviour, significance of contribution. The results showed that the highest rankings by researchers had not been heard of by managers, and that the researchers were most concerned with such aspects as experimental control and verifiability, while this emphasis was absent from the preferences of the managers.

How, then, can the practitioner and the sponsor collaborate? The sponsor is rarely interested in acquiring the knowledge of the practitioner, though he may be interested in selected facets and particular techniques. Practitioners may under-rate the selective nature of management's approach. An executive of a leading European firm reported: 'In 1968 we thought like Herzberg, in 1969 like Shepherd, in 1970 like Beckard, and I think it's Tannenbaum for 1971.' The lack of deep interest of sponsors is reflected in the predominance of engineering and peritus models (see Sections 7.2, 7.3). In a similar way the practitioner may not, and cannot, communicate his complete definition of valid knowledge to the sponsor. This leads to a distinction between the practitioner's own analytical frameworks and those he presents to the sponsor.

Given that the practitioner faces the problem of relating the behavioural science perspective to the sponsor's practical problems, then it should be acknowledged that the practitioner faces a number of difficulties. The practitioner's actual analysis of problems might be perceived by the sponsor as critical or threatening, when his objective is simply to map the existing situation. We can postulate that the problems of the practitioner will be least in industrial enterprises, especially the scientifically based industries, and greatest in enterprises characterized by distinctive ideologies (e.g. the military and labour unions). Whatever the context, the practitioner faces the problem of making his competence and activities intelligible to the layman. It seems clear (Clark and Ford, 1970) that practitioners have developed general frameworks which are used as linking devices between the sponsor's problems and the practitioner's skills and these presenting frameworks should not be interpreted as the actual diagnostic perspective used by the practitioner. For example, it is hard to imagine sponsors who would readily accept the recommendations for diagnosis presented in the analytic frameworks of the contingency theorists. In effect, what is presented to the sponsor is the end product of the practitioner's application of his special perspective. Mayo (1947) makes an apparently similar distinction when he separates 'knowledge of acquaintance' from 'knowledge about'. The former comes from the direct experience of particular situations, and we have pointed to its importance in applied research programmes. It includes skills that differ from general knowledge in that they are manifested at a particular point as a manipulative dexterity based on the handling of people and things. Hence knowledge of acquaintance is difficult to transmit, is never truly articulate, and is only slowly disseminated. In contrast, 'knowledge about' is the product of reflective and abstract thinking. Its universal features make it easier to transmit. Mayo argues that knowledge of acquaintance is inadequately developed in the social sciences. Organizational development can be seen as an effort to tackle just the problem identified by Mayo, although its method is distinctive. It is based upon a careful selection of propositions and concepts about human behaviour in relation to certain specific goals (e.g. risk taking relationships) and it has developed a technology for connecting the knowledge of the situation to reflective knowledge.

Gouldner has suggested that the practitioner can use the device of the 'lay hypothesis' to establish valid knowledge with the sponsor. This involves the practitioner's accepting certain ideas held by the sponsor and formulating them into questions rather than statements of fact. For example, the sponsor may wish to introduce a delegated form of organization, requiring high commitment to the job by those affected, and requiring a willingness by those currently occupying positions of influence to accept a levelling of the hierarchy. The sponsor believes that this can be done, but the practitioner's analysis suggests a number of complicating factors. The practitioner may then work with the sponsor to identify the assumptions underlying the preference for delegated decision making, and then formulate these assumptions into a series of hypotheses about what conditions must exist for the favoured idea to work. The practitioner then carries out investigations to establish whether these conditions do exist. This may seem a complex way of operating. However, Gouldner contends that the practitioner has to undertake activities which are seemingly scientifically senseless but actually sociologically sensible.

The distinction between analytical and presenting frameworks has an important implication for the understanding of the activities and ideologies of the practitioner. Sociologists have, with certain notable exceptions (e.g. Bendix, 1956), tended to neglect this distinction.*

6.2 Practitioners and scientists

It is now convenient to develop, in somewhat exaggerated form, some distinctions between the practitioner's perspective on valid knowledge and that of the behavioural scientist.†

A typification of the practitioner would be as follows:

– He is essentially an artist operating with knowledge of acquaintance and knowledge about
– He adopts a diagnostic orientation to the sponsor's problems and deals with specific cases
– He accepts an incomplete prediction and is not in search of origins
– His focus of the capta is upon that which can be manipulated and is socially legitimate
– His emphasis is upon variables that can be controlled
– He views the layman as a source of hypothesis to be tested in the particular context
– He is not a detached observer
– He seeks to obtain sanctions from the sponsor rather than be concerned with explanation and understanding

This typification raises a number of problems; for example, it is questionable to assert that the practitioner should be concerned *only*

---

* The possibilities for a more thorough and significant analysis are indicated in the studies of ideology by Geertz, 1964, and Sartori, 1969. This is an important area for research since it provides an insight into changing arenas of social conflict – see F. H. Marx, 1968.

† Based upon contributions to the volume of readings edited by Bennis, Benne and Chin, *The Planning of Change*, 1969 edition.

with variables which can be manipulated. It may be argued that an action research project's most significant achievement could be to change the sponsor's understanding of the problem. It also raises the difficult issue of the selection of concepts by practitioners while not fully exploring the latent social functions of knowledge. Finally, it raises a number of concerns about the claims of practitioners to contribute to the theory and interests of the academic community. This is not to deny the possibility, but the exigencies of the practitioner's role do not provide the most favourable setting for research. We may now contrast the typification of the practitioner with that of the behavioural scientist engaged in basic research.

- His emphasis is upon knowledge about, and he is somewhat scornful of knowledge of acquaintance
- He adopts an emphasis upon exploration in order to formulate hypotheses
- He is concerned with hypothesis and verification
- He prefers more complete prediction and searches for origins
- The capta includes all variables which are theoretically relevant irrespective of controllability
- The layman is rarely a source of hypothesis
- The scientist is expected to be a detached observer
- The researcher is concerned with explanation and understanding

Essentially, the scientist is not, in this typification, a purveyor of certainty. He reveals rather than mystifies.

Though oversimplified, the typifications do highlight some of the differences between scientists and practitioners. The perspective of the scientists is generated and sustained within the scientific community where the planning and undertaking of research is judged within stated rules of social control governing the formulation of problems, the means used to test explanations and carry out observations, and the format of presenting findings to colleagues. The scientist works in a system where his perspective on theoretical problems, with all its nuances, is comprehended by colleagues. Hence his strategy for obtaining the incorporation of his researches into the stock of knowledge of the community stresses rational means. Although this characterization is too normative, and neglects the controversies surrounding discoveries (see Kuhn, 1970), it does suggest that the extension of the rational strategies of the academic outside the scientific community may not be successful – the rules of the game in non-academic settings are overtly less open and rational.

In contrast to the scientist, the practitioner is typically working within the same 'net of association', the same shared meanings, as the sponsoring organization. He must judge personally when to make cognitive inputs. The difficulties involved may be noted from the emphasis given to the role of the sponsor's values in determining outcomes to action research. Emery and Trist (1963) emphasize the 'maturity' of the value system, and Jones highlights the relevance of 'client receptivity', suggesting that its importance is greater than has been supposed. Thus the problem for the practitioner in managing knowledge is to maintain a distinctive contribution and still stay in business.

This difference in emphasis between practice and science is important. Benne, Chin and Bennis (1969) state that claims for 'the utility of scientific findings for practitioners must take account of this important distinction between the two orientations'. They suggest that it is in the diagnostic phase of action research that the practitioner finds the most direct use for scientific generalizations. This is because the generalizations 'point to meaningful connections between variables possibly at work within any situation being analysed'.

6.3 Role of theory

Practitioners are somewhat reluctant to state that they are using particular theories. (This may well reflect the fact that managers frequently refer to behavioural scientists as 'theorists' in the hope that they can jokingly cajole the practitioner.) Revans argues that we should use the minimum of theory, but I would wish to disagree. I feel that we should recognize an important distinction between the use of theory by the practitioner to diagnose and interpret and the material that he actually presents to and shares with the sponsor. Thus we should look at the kinds of theory that the practitioner utilizes and the role of theory in action research. Interestingly enough, D. McGregor wrote *The Human Side of Enterprise* to emphasize the role of theory. Although his thinking, especially Theory x and Theory y, is widely known, few are aware of this aspect of his work.

On the nature of theory and its role as a set of interconnected meanings, Einstein observed that 'it needed great imagination to realize that it was not the charges, not the particles, but the field in the space in between the charges and particles which is central for a description of physical phenomena.'

It is convenient to distinguish four types of theory (Golembiewski, 1961) and examine their part in action research.

1. *Ethical theory* deals with desirable rather than actual occurrences and is exemplified by the Ten Commandments.
2. *Utopian theory* deals with an aspect of the empirical world, and is thus distinguished from ethical theory. It is insensitive to empirical data, either because its propositions cannot be tested or because they are not revised in the light of empirical evidence. Classical organization theory is a good example. The propositions are constructs of the imagination which do not need empirical counterparts. The choice of propositions is unlimited, but their treatment is ruled by logic. They may, however, aid the development of empirical theory.
3. *Empirical theory* is a statement of what is related to what, and may be contrasted with beliefs although there are logical similarities. Essentially an empirical theory's utility is its ability to predict accurately the outcomes of similar events and related phenomena. One problem is that a theory may predict for the wrong reasons, but empirical theory can benefit the practice of organizational change. One basic problem in empirical theory is the isolation of 'similar phenomena' which describe the real world.
4. *Goal-based empirical theory* is built upon empirical theory, but it is not concerned with 'what is'. The focus is upon 'what must be done in order to achieve what is desired'. The theory is in two parts. First, a decision on what is desired. This is based upon a value or norm, which can be challenged at the level of its acceptability and is the goal. Examples include creating a risk-taking atmosphere, participative management, and centralized control. Second there is the survey of empirical theory to determine what conditions must exist for the goal selected to exist. The crucial question is, Does the theory reflect a knowledge of the empirical world sufficient to warrant a reasonable expectation that following the theory will achieve the desired end?

An excellent example of a goal-based empirical theory is to be found in the theorizing of Perrow, which is directed toward matching the organizational structure with the nature of the tasks being undertaken by the enterprise to transform its raw material into finished product. Raw material can refer to symbols, to things and to people. Perrow's own researches have been concentrated on hospitals and correctional institutions, but he incorporates the empirical researches undertaken in a wide variety of contexts, including industry, education and the military. His is essentially a bottom up type of theory in so far as he argues that the practitioner should make a profile of the tasks undertaken to transform the basic raw material by measuring the four dimensions: stability of raw material, knowledge of raw material, frequency with which exceptions occur, and the method of solving them. In instances where the raw material, let us say, recruits into a volunteer army, is stable and unvarying, where it creates a few exceptions, and those which do occur are easily analysable and answered, then the theory would state that there was a low degree of uncertainty for those persons transforming the raw material. A low degree of uncertainty can be managed quite efficiently by an organizational structure characterized by a high degree of fragmentation of jobs which can be coordinated by predetermined production programming – that is to say, by a structure in which there is a hierarchy of authority, expertise, and power. However, as the nature of the raw material changes, let us say the incoming generation are enlisted men who prefer democratic authority styles, then those responsible for induction will find that their existing knowledge is inadequate for dealing with the exceptions that arise. According to the theory we should adapt the structure to create a less hierarchical ordering of decision taking until the key characteristics of the new populations are identified and control strategies are devised and applied (see Perrow, 1970).

Perrow's theorizing, illustrated by the small fragment presented above, represents one of the important contributions to what is known as the contingency theory of organizational structure. The value of the concepts and propositions in this approach is that they sensitize the practitioner to critical aspects of the sponsor's situation and context and provide him with a repertoire of ideas for analysis and the devising of solutions.

In practice the practitioner, like the good basic researcher, should be eclectic (see Denzin, 1970); it may well be necessary to devise new concepts and to reformulate existing ones. A sound knowledge of theory is significant for the action researcher because this guides his selection of problems and their interpretation. It also provides the point of reference for the development of knowledge about organizational change.

Summary

In defining valid knowledge we have emphasized the role given to theory and have distinguished between the practitioner's diagnostic analysis and the more generalized frameworks utilized to present the diagnosis to sponsors. This distinction is of considerable relevance because a number of sociologists have mistakenly assumed that these presenting frameworks are to be equated with analytical perspectives.

Practitioners are concerned with problems of change and tend to specialize in tackling particular problems. This emphasis is reflected in the choice of goal. In important respects the choice includes assumptions and beliefs which the practitioner has about the place of man in society, and we have thus termed this emphasis, or posture, the practitioner's *focus*. It is likely that some of the controversies among practitioners about the relevance of particular change strategies stem from differences in the choice of focus. Further, it is more than likely that the choice of focus influences the selection of means for implementing the goal.

Although we have exaggerated the differences between the orientations of scientists and practitioners, this does have the important advantage of highlighting the fact that the scientist is typically concerned to convince scientists and the practitioner is concerned to convince the intelligent layman.

CHAPTER 7

Collaborative role relationships

Role refers to the behaviour and beliefs of the practitioner with respect to the extent to which the relationship with the sponsor should be characterized by the sharing of initiatives and directives. Practitioners have basic postures, predominant styles, that can be identified along a continuum of relative influence in making policy decisions about the action research. The two poles of the continuum represent the interests of high mutual influence on the one hand and unilateral influence on the other. The practitioner will occupy varying positions along the continuum on different occasions, but it is possible to identify preferences of style which the practitioner believes are appropriate for achieving change in the client enterprise. These preferred roles form an important area of enquiry for our analysis. We must ask: what are the major roles preferred by practitioners and what evidence is there about their relative appropriateness to organizational change?

One of the major concerns of practitioners has been that of creating the appropriate relationship for dealing with sponsors' problems (see Lippitt *et al.*, 1958; Sofer, 1961; Bennis, 1966). Although we know remarkably little about the ways in which practitioners actually operate in making their diagnoses and applying their strategies for intervening in particular situations (see Trist, 1968), we see in the published accounts of professionals a striking preference for a collaborative relationship with sponsors – it is recognized by the mutual setting of the goals of the assignment (see Bennis, 1969). This preference is most evident in the activities of those involved in organizational development; they are particularly concerned with what Leavitt called the people variable. However, it is apparent from the case studies (Chapter Four) that there are practitioners whose activities do not easily fit into the collaborative mode. Does this mean that they are wrong?

The work of O'Connell, which we examined in Section 4.2, challenges the generality of the collaborative model and emphasizes the importance of delineating just what the collaborative model states and how other models differ. For example, there are certain similarities between the preference of Bennis for collaboration, of Schein (1969) for the process model, and of Gouldner (1961) for the clinical model. The general appropriateness of the collaborative model is challenged by O'Connell's study of the management consultant. He terms the consultant's role model the 'peritus', arguing that it is exemplified by a preference for behaving as an expert. Another possibility for unilateral influence arises when the sponsor takes the initiatives and purchases answers to problems that he has defined and believes are adequately defined. The general term for this role relationship is that of the engineering model as described by Gouldner.

We shall begin our study of role relationships by examining those models which approximate to a collaborative relationship, then we shall discuss the engineering model, and finally the peritus, or expert, model. As before, we should be open-minded in our approach, preferring to discover what each model contains and seeking for consistent patterns. The selection of the appropriate role relationship should be based upon the problem territory and the state of the sponsoring system.

7.1 Collaborative model

The collaborative model, which is the one most favoured by Bennis, is to be recognized by a relationship between the practitioner and sponsor which is one of joint effort, where there is a mutual determination of goals, and in which each party has equal opportunity to influence the other. Problem solving is conducted in a 'spirit of inquiry' where the voluntary relationship can be concluded by either party. In suggesting this model, Bennis has in mind that it is particularly relevant to the problems of interpersonal relations. The collaborative model facilitates the introduction of valid knowledge about interpersonal relationships and Bennis is implicitly suggesting that these cannot be introduced by strategies which rely upon power and coercion or are biased to rational and empirical strategies (see Chin and Benne, 1969).

Collaboration may be contrasted with models in which goal setting is non-deliberate, or one sided (e.g. the sponsor sets the goals and is dominant). It may be noted that Bennis is not questioning the existence of other models, but he severely doubts their relevance to the problems and focus he has defined as central.

Schein (1969) prefers a perspective which he calls the process model. In this perspective the diagnosis is interpreted as a joint affair, and the consultant is willing to enter the enterprise without a clear mission or need. Schein defines the process model very largely as a set of activities undertaken by the practitioner which are directed towards assisting the sponsor to perceive, understand, and to act upon events which occur in the sponsor's environment. The underlying assumptions include the recognition that the manager may not know the problem, or be able to articulate it; that managers do not necessarily know how to use the practitioner; that joint working is both economical of diagnostic time and also assists the sponsor to learn how to recognize similar problems when they appear again.

The preference by action researchers for a continuing and collaborative relationship is echoed in the analysis of Gouldner, who proposes the clinical model. He illustrates this model by reference to Holmberg's (1963) study, which was an episode within a wider study of an Indian community at the Hacienda Vicos in Peru. The specific problem was that of strife, fights and disagreements amongst the Indians over the ownership of cattle. The solution devised by the social scientists was remarkably simple and very reminiscent of Whyte's (1949) technological solution for conflicts between waitresses and kitchen staff in an American hotel. In the instance of the Indians, the suggested device was branding the cattle. This was discussed with the leaders and in a general assembly, but it was adopted only after the wealthier leaders agreed to have their cattle branded first. Gouldner notes that the social scientist did not accept the definition of the problem as presented, but interpreted this as only one of the symptoms. Their diagnosis produced a novel and simple solution.

This example illustrates the importance of diagnosis (see also Lawrence and Lorsch, 1969), and the existence of this, coupled with mutual-problem definition, as distinctive features of the clinical model. The practitioner is also involved in the articulation of the problem and in a continuous relationship. Another distinctive feature is that the interface between the sponsoring system and *other subject populations* is taken as part of the action research. This point was also evident in the Paterson study (see Section 4.2) and in the organizational design project at CCE Ltd (see Section 4.4). A final aspect of interest is that the exponent of the clinical model does not expect his findings to be acceptable because they have been acquired by applying the 'best canons of scientific research', but expects some opposition and conflict with the sponsor.

7.2 Engineering model

In Gouldner's exposition of the engineering model, the sponsor requests the practitioner, for example, to conduct a survey of employee morale. The terms of the request are largely accepted as given and investigators are sent out to collect the information required. It is then analysed and compiled into a report which is sent to the sponsor. The typical report contains large sections of facts and some recommendations. A member of the agency may then visit the sponsor to discuss some of the findings. Gouldner suggests that the report will be dispatched to some dusty shelf and its conclusions forgotten. He suggests that the engineering model pervades the transactions between behavioural scientists and policy makers. This point would seem to be well supported by Lyons's analysis, though he seems less critical about the arrangement (Lyons, 1968). Gouldner suggests that the principle assumption adopted by the sponsor is that problems arise from a lack of information and that the role of practitioner is therefore to produce information. He suggests a certain irony in a situation where the utilitarian notions are being expunged from social theories yet should be so central to the way in which applied behavioural science workers see their role. More emphatically, Gouldner asserts that practitioners who accept the engineering model are especially vulnerable to an 'unwitting redefinition of their roles in ways which obliterate their professional distinctiveness and identity', and he cites policy formation in the military sector to illustrate this point. Lang (1969), in an overview of military sociology, strongly supports the suggestion that the role of established psychologists has become heavily routinized and somewhat constrained. In Gouldner's commentary on the military it is suggested that the practitioner's problem is that although the adoption of the language of military thinking may be functional for close relations with the military elite, its fruitfulness for the development of action research is more doubtful.

7.3 Peritus model

The peritus model is the one proposed by O'Connell (see Section 4.2) to describe the behaviour of the management consultant at the Leeds

Insurance Company. In the early stages of the relationship with the sponsor, the consultant undertook a diagnosis, supervised a number of pilot tests, and, when dealing with top management, used the power of fact and rational argument to gain a commitment for change. Many of the executives contributed to the analysis. They were not mere data sources but were in a dialogue with the consultant in the pre-report stage and in the formulation of the action programme. In contrast, the managers who were part of the subject population had little influence on the proposed changes. The consultant used the authority of expertise, with a little participation from the sponsor, to gain commitment for change. O'Connell suggests that a sufficient number of the executives felt committed and could identify with the consultant. Later, following pilot demonstrations of the proposed system, the consultant handed the selling of the new system to the company's operating executives, and so the new system was identified by the target populations as a company product. The consultant did not collaborate with the client in the sense frequently used by social scientists, but performed as an experienced expert and acted as a man who was expected to advise what to do and how to do it. Also, the consultant focused upon the client system as an ineffective technical system rather than as a social system, although he demonstrated a keen awareness of local political issues and nuances.

Summary

It is evident that there are considerable similarities between the collaborative, process, and clinical models – all three are typified by mutual definition of the problem and an approximately equal power relationship between the practitioner and the sponsor. For the purposes of convenience we shall adopt Bennis's term of collaborative relationship.

The two remaining models are essentially unilateral. In the case of the engineering relationship, it is the sponsor who is dominant; in the case of the peritus relationship, it is the practitioner.

We may summarize by adopting three basic models. These are the collaborative model, the engineering model, and the peritus model. There is no disagreement among either practitioners or researchers about the actual existence of these three models, but there are important preferences which we have already identified. The question which now arises is whether one model is more appropriate than another. Some practitioners and researchers would argue that the relationship and intervention strategy must be selected on the basis of the problem and situation rather than on a general commitment to one model (e.g. peritus); we shall examine this particular argument further in Chapter 10.

CHAPTER 8

Intervention strategies

Intervention strategy refers to the means utilized by practitioners to achieve organizational change. We noted that practitioners have to convince an audience of intelligent laymen of the appropriateness of their recommendations. This means that the selection of manipulable variables must be done in a manner that provides the practitioner with the opportunity to make plans for the changes required. There are a variety of possible ways of proceeding. The commanding officer on the airfield in the Paterson study (Section 4.5) attempted to obtain a change in morale by giving a pep talk to the fliers, but Paterson found a more effective strategy by using his own role to implant a symbolic enemy which became the target for externalizing the frustrations and aggressions that had developed. Paterson's covert strategy may be contrasted with the delegated problem-solving approach of Revans (4.1) and the group problem-solving approach that I used at CCE (4.4).

From the cases presented in Chapter 4, and from the discussions that proceeded from them, we can see that there are a number of important ways in which intervention strategies vary. From these we shall select three for special examination of the following: the degree of directiveness of the strategy; the relative emphasis upon experiential or conceptual methods; the theory of phases in action research.

8.1 Directive or non-directive?

The case study by O'Connell provides a sharp contrast of approach to those adopted by Revans and by myself. O'Connell's study shows the consultant initiating the direction of the change programme and is thus an example of high directness; Revans's case is essentially an example of a delegated approach, and the method utilized in CCE of the short-life project groups and joint working with the Azimuth Group is also non-directive but is a joint method of working. Strong elements of non-directive strategies can be seen in the work of

Hjelholt, suggesting that he conceives the nature of changes in the social system implied by certain new technologies to be so fundamental that the dissemination of information and conventional training would not be sufficient. The emphasis is upon facilitating the emergence of a new 'role-culture' which would incorporate certain features of the existing system, such as the role of the captain as an arbitrator. Thus the conferences that Hjelholt used began an erosion of the existing social ties between members of the crew as the first stage in moving the members of the conference to a new position in which role boundaries would be more blurred than in the past and the status system less sharply hierarchized. The 'dry land' rehearsals provided the framework for this new role-culture, and Hjelholt travelled on the tanker to check its implementation. Again we note a strong non-directive element in the application of the second and subsequent phases of the Managerial Grid at Sigma and in the subtle use of indirect manipulation of symbols by Paterson.

An interesting development in non-directive approaches is the one-day confrontation meeting developed by Beckhard (1967) and now being used to an increasing extent. P. J. Chartrand (1972), an in-house practitioner working within the Canadian public bureaucracies, has provided a fascinating account of how this strategy can be applied. Its relevance is sufficiently general to justify the inclusion here of a brief outline of the mechanics of the confrontation meeting.

The confrontation meeting was designed by Beckhard to provide a diagnosis and partial solution to a very basic set of problems that faces many sponsors, that it is always difficult to obtain an accurate picture of how the members of the enterprise are reacting to change. This problem is particularly acute in periods of crisis, when there is frequently confusion and usually less opportunity for communication within management and between management and other groups. Beckhard's suggested solution is to take a quick measure which is taken as the basis for action plans, all in a matter of hours. This intervention strategy provides a microreading of the existing situation as perceived by members of the enterprise and then involves everyone in the interpretation of the situation and the devising of solutions that arise out of widespread commitment. An example is set out in Table 8.1.

The joint problem approach implied in Beckhard may be compared with the expert approach evident in the job enrichment studies. The expert approach, typified by directness, is frequently criticized as

G

TABLE 8.1 *A one-day confrontation meeting*

Phase	Time	Activity	Summary
1	45–60 minutes	Senior manager communicates his goals for the meeting.	Setting climate
2	1 hour	Group divides into small hetero-geneous syndicates who identify current problems, which are recorded by an elected reporter.	Collecting information
3	1 hour	Reporters summarize main points on newsprint. These are categorized and duplicated for general distribution.	Sharing information
4	1 hour 15 minutes	After 15 minutes in the general meeting, members convene with problem list in functional groups to discuss problems, decide priorities, identify issues for top management, and decide how to communicate the results to subordinates.	Setting priority and group action planning
5	1–2 hours	General session in which the groups from Phase 4 report their findings. Top management responds and agrees on priorities.	Planning organizational action
6	1–3 hours	Top-management team meets separately to plan follow-up actions, which are reported back to the whole group in a few days.	Follow-up by top team
7	2 hours	Follow-up by all concerned some 4 to 6 weeks later.	Progress review

Based on R. Beckhard, (Confrontation Meeting). In Dalton, Lawrence, & Greiner (1970), pp. 270–280.

ineffective in achieving its objectives, but our case studies and analyses indicate that the criticism should either be rejected or at least specified more precisely. For example, it is quite clear that Paul and Robertson were able to achieve important changes in intrinsic satisfaction and performance (see Section 4.6). How then can we state categorically that this strategy is ineffective?

We have remarked at several points on the consensus amongst practitioners against direct approaches. It is therefore of particular interest to note the analysis made by Hutte of the most effective manner of operating for the consultant practitioner.* His observations are based upon experience in a number of situations, including experimental changes in the structure of group organization and interrelationships introduced into the post, cheque and clearing departments of the Dutch Postal, Telegraph & Telephone Company, in the mid-1950's.† Hutte's emphasis is upon the way in which direct interventions by practitioners can facilitate the adaptation of enterprises to the problems arising from growth. He suggests that the practitioner should start by mapping the strategic power centres in the sponsoring enterprise to identify the integer power centre. This map reveals what Hutte terms the 'strategic pathway': it guides the consultant in ensuring that key perspectives and information are distributed in a manner that retains the involvement of the dominant coalitions.

How can we resolve the question whether the practitioner's intervention strategies should be directive or non-directive? I believe that we should not expect the practitioner to commit himself to one style rather than another without bearing in mind the *focus* of the intervention and the *organizational context*. In situations where the practitioner's focus is the creation of more positive relationships within a problem-solving group, it would seem strange to impose this by direct methods in the British and American cultures. It might, however, be effective in some kinds of bureaucratic setting (cf. Bennis, 1969) and in some cultures.

8.2 Experiential or conceptual?

The use of the behavioural sciences in organizations has developed in three historical phases. In the first phase, there was a strong element of teaching and preaching about the advantages of styles of authority

---

* H. Hutte, 1968, *The Sociatry of Work*. This work, which is of considerable relevance, is unfortunately only published in Dutch. The interpretation is mine.

† Interestingly, these experiments were undertaken in work situations similar to those examined by Crozier, 1964. The characteristics of the tasks seem as similar as Perrow would suggest, thus indicating that the specific cultural interpretation by Crozier may be misplaced in this instance.

that were supportive and general rather than coercive and specific. Although the teachers were somewhat unsuccessful in conveying this message to groups of managers on short courses, especially in the human relations tradition, it does seem that the move towards more manipulative styles has proceeded. In the second phase, conventional teaching methods were attacked for being individual in focus and rational in assumption. That is to say, critics, armed with the depressing results of knowledge transfer produced by evaluation research, argued that the strategy was too preoccupied with changing the attitudes of individuals in the classroom situation and that the sharp discrepancy between the classroom and the workplace eroded any potential benefits. By this time the group methods of changing behaviour and attitudes, given prominence by social psychologists, had become fashionable. Coupled with the group emphasis was the swing to learning by experiencing. Thus it was argued that the best means for learning about group processes was, for example, to experience the situation of an unstructured group in its first and subsequent stages (if there were any). In this way, advocates of experiential learning argued, the practitioner (i.e. trainer) could intervene at carefully chosen times to provide a conceptual clarification which would be meaningful because it would be related to behaviours that had been observed and felt moments earlier. The group approach with its experiential tone was transformed into what became known as systemic strategies (see Katz and Kahn, 1966, chap. 13). The systemic experiential approach is currently dominant, but there is already an awareness of a need for more emphasis on the conceptual tool kit of the manager, especially the concepts he uses to examine the social–organizational aspects. This is the third phase.

This new stage overlaps with the systemic experiential phase and is characterized by an emphasis upon the role of concepts and propositions about human behaviour as a storehouse or repertoire of understanding about ways in which organizational systems must be constantly reconciled to what is happening to the technology and the external environment. Advocates of the conceptual approach argue that managers cannot learn about the organizational perspective from group experiences, yet this knowledge is important. Thus the major debate today is between the *systemically experiential* and the *systemically conceptual* perspectives.

The systemically experiential approach is focused upon the people variable, not only because it is a key variable from within the interacting schema of Leavitt, but in the belief that it requires and is susceptible to improvement by the methods adopted. The method of intervention relies heavily on giving the sponsor and subject populations direct experience of situations that are outside their normal experience of training. The freshly created group composed of a diagonal slice of members and placed in a room together off-site for the first time represents a simple example. In this strategy emphasis is given to the direct involvement of the client system in working out the programme of change through a dialogic relation that reveals the differences between the ways in which the practitioner and the sponsor perceive the problems. The strategy is based on the belief that the major difficulty facing the sponsor lies in attitudes, values, norms, and the internal and external relationships of the sponsoring system. Its tone is essentially educative, relying on the here-and-now experience of both sponsor and practitioner to diagnose the problem and reveal potential solutions. Thus practitioners in the systemic experiential approach believe that the people variable is as important to over-all performance as material technology, and that the clarification and reconstruction of values is of pivotal importance in achieving change. The practitioner aims to get the existing value system out into the open in order to work through value conflicts within the sponsoring system and between the practitioner and the sponsor. In some accounts of this approach there is a tendency to assume that the only important value conflicts exist between the practitioner who understands reality and the sponsor who does not and is recalcitrant. Exponents of this position are in effect covert experts like Paterson, but it is clear that the dialogue implied in the experiential approach should include content as well as the relationship. I would argue strongly against the idea that the experiential approach should be aimed at getting changes accepted by group methods and contend that the requirements of organizational change do in effect require the integration of a multiplicity of approaches from the existing internal professional groups, as used in CCE (see Section 4.4).

Exponents of the systemically conceptual approach do not advocate teaching as the single best way of achieving organizational change, but they do emphasize that teaching has an important part to play in the diffusion of concepts to sponsors.* Without these concepts the

* See especially Chapple and Sayles, 1961; Zaleznik and Moment, 1964; Seiler, 1967; Lawrence and Lorsch, 1969; P. A. Clark, 1972.

sponsor cannot readily identify those problems which are particularly amenable to the work of the organizational analyst. Here again we can detect some impatience with the sponsor's antecedent state by those closely involved in creating organizational change. Later, we shall examine this aspect when looking at the diffusion model of knowledge dissemination and utilization (see Chapter 12). Its significance is reflected in interpretation of the relative success of the strategy adopted in CCE Ltd, which took account of the fact that key members of the sponsoring system had an awareness and knowledge of recent developments in the use of behavioural sciences in organizations and had visited ongoing experiments.

The role of key individuals is somewhat slighted in the criticisms by exponents of both systemic approaches on the place of teaching, seminars, and similar activities. To neglect the influence of individuals is in effect to adopt a definition of the concept of role that is sharply at variance with our current understanding of the individual's strategies in occupying particular roles (see Goffman, 1961; Levinson, 1959; Weick, 1970).

We now turn from an overview of the emergence of the systemic intervention strategies to examine the problem of sharing concepts with the sponsor. How much of the conceptual and theoretical frameworks of the practitioner does the sponsor need to understand in order to make the optimum use of action research? In the case of Paterson, the answer is very little; the significant feature of the Paterson study is that he carved out a role and problem territory without this being fully recognized by the members of the RAF station. Both Hjelholt and I occupied a somewhat similar position, but it was formally recognized. However, in none of these three cases is there extensive evidence of reliance upon a heavy explicit conceptual input. By this we mean that the practitioners did not rely upon extensive sharing of their own diagnostic and problem frameworks, but rather sought to use general frameworks which contained and highlighted variables and concepts of direct relevance to the specific sponsor. A good example is my use of sociotechnical analysis where this framework was publicly stressed in the early phases to emphasize the interdependence of the social and technical systems and to establish a political rationale for the inclusion of a mixture of specialisms in the short-life project groups. The details of the actual diagnostic frameworks were revealed only in so far as it was necessary to ensure that these groups focused upon issues that were of relevance to the design of the new organization. The low visibility of conceptual inputs is also reflected in Revans's emphasis upon a minimum of theory. Again, when I was interviewing some Dutch social scientists, a young and very bright organizational psychologist explained the in-house research programme by reference to the big names of behavioural science, although earlier he had indicated doubts about the basis of their theories. He then added that the theories of A and B were used 'to propel our own programme forward'.

One of the important ways in which the practitioner can work directly with the sponsor to examine the sponsor's conception of the existing situation and of the factors which are moulding it is to take some of the explanations that the intelligent layman advocates and formulate them as hypotheses to be tested. This strategy, given the title of 'lay hypothesis' by Gouldner, represents a useful manner of dealing with the fact that the practitioner is continually presented with the sponsor's definition of the problems and that these explanations cannot be easily ignored. The lay hypothesis transforms a difficulty into an advantage. An example of this strategy is contained in my work on the design of the work situation for female packing crews in CCE. In that instance, the sponsoring group believed that they would be able to introduce a form of organizing that would provide more opportunity for decision making. Our diagnosis had indicated that the existing situation had the desired attributes and the proposed technological solutions would in effect remove them. We designed a piece of investigation to discover jointly what were the actual and proposed situations. In this way we tested the assumptions held by part of the sponsoring group about what existed and what could be introduced.

We have stressed the importance of a concept-based analysis but have argued that the sponsor does not require all the same kinds of knowledge as the practitioner. Given that cognitive inputs are of some importance, how does the practitioner handle cognitive inputs to the sponsor?

There are several aspects to this question (see Bowers, 1970). The first aspect we may consider is the problem of who makes the conceptual analysis. Should it be the sponsor or the practitioner? In much of the non-directive training of a group kind, the members of the group are expected to construct their own conceptual frameworks for understanding the group processes, receiving help from the trainer. It is highly unlikely that the equivalent of Paterson's methetic theory of group roles and relations would emerge from this do-it-yourself approach. Undoubtedly the exponents of the non-directive approaches to organizational change have placed themselves in a position that is easy to misunderstand! However, we must note that the goal of their work is frequently the change from impersonal relations to more authentic interpersonal interaction. The empirical theory on which they draw is derived from experiments with leadership styles and similar studies, much of which apparently lends support to the non-directive stance. Hence, we may argue that their approach to conceptual inputs is at least consistent with the theory. Whether that theory is adequate is, of course, another matter, but it may be recognized that practitioners assume a relationship between the relevance of conceptual inputs and the kinds of solution involved. Some believe that there is a higher relevance in organizational projects than in interpersonal training.

The second aspect of conceptual inputs concerns their *form*.

Earlier, we distinguished some forms by the degree of formalization. For example, the Management Grid situation is highly formalized. Each member is required to undertake a given amount of reading and pre-study of the theory and rationale for the Grid. This is reinforced by the structured exercises based upon measuring dimensions which are central to the theory, such as the extent of task-centred leadership. Similarly, the technology developed for implementing the Job Enrichment theories was highly formalized. In contrast, there was low formalization in the work of Paterson, Revans, and Clark. The extent of formalization strongly influences the relationship between the practitioner and the sponsor.

The third aspect concerns the *timing* of the inputs. Here there are wide differences in practice. The topic is particularly controversial and is likely to remain so for some time because the approaches of practitioners, even when highly formalized as in the Management Grid, are personal interpretations of 'what is wrong' with the organization. Though practitioners would deny the point, it is hard for the onlooker to draw any conclusion other than that many of the new technologies (e.g. organizational development) are presented as though they were general panaceas. The controversies will only be resolved as the amount of comparative research on the same approaches to change are undertaken. Thus we might reasonably expect to find that many of the variations in timing are quite rational when examined in light of the objectives of the action research project. We must not assume, for example, that the objectives of the seven cases presented in Chapter 4 were similar.

Timing of inputs can be (a) in the form of an initial input; (b) as each stage of a project is completed; (c) at the end of an assignment as part of the implementation phases; (d) over time in a diffused manner. An important point for the practitioner to bear in mind when making judgements about timing is the interest and requirements of the sponsor. Action research is not an alternative method of injecting the contents of university courses into the thinking of executives; it is a highly discriminated activity undertaken by professionals who have a special competence and intend to practice in the problem territory of organizational change. Additionally, we know from studies of sponsors that they do not share the same preoccupations as practitioners. B. Appleby and J. R. Ford have shown from a survey of industry-based applied work and also university-based work that the common ground between practitioners and sponsors is limited. Given this situation, the practitioner must choose carefully how much of a conceptual input is required and when is the best time.

There has undoubtedly been a strong assumption in the writing of practitioners that moments of crisis or conflict provide the best opportunities for cognitive inputs. In my own experience and researches, I find a good deal of evidence to contradict this assertion. Rather than commit practitioners to the rule of attempting to use (or even create) crises, it is better to think in terms of introducing the conceptualization when the time is judged appropriate. A very important point, and one which is much neglected, is the length of time it takes before a sponsoring group is fully able to grasp and utilize such cognitive inputs as the practitioners inject. It is a matter of several years, not months.

So far we have stressed both the relevance of conceptual inputs and also the problems of undertaking them given that sponsors have only a limited interest and requirement. This raises the problem of balance between necessity and extent. Since conceptual inputs cannot be experienced so readily with respect to socio-organizational behaviour as they can with intra-group behaviour, how can the problem be resolved? Two lines of development are most obviously available. First, a minimum basic conceptual apparatus is likely to be needed by and presented to the sponsor, overlapping with the competences of the practitioner. This is required so that the sponsor can identify problem situations and engage in a meaningful dialogue. Second, given the first situation we have in effect created a problem territory (see Section 3.2) for the practitioner, and the next stage is to ensure the availability of practitioners to undertake the solution of problems. Thus the role of the behavioural scientist requires institutionalization within the sponsoring system.

The stress on conceptual inputs has in effect been a stress on what are sometimes called the *rational-empirical approaches* to systemic change. It has been implied that these are generally ineffective, particularly by exponents of the group methods focusing on the improvement of interpersonal competence. In response to such criticisms, I have argued that the *systemic conceptual* approaches incorporate the full range of interacting variables suggested by Leavitt. My argument does not directly challenge the relevance of the experiential approaches in organizational development at the group level, and the Managerial Grid may be regarded as a formalized intervention strategy with a built-in selection of conceptual tools. Implicitly my argument states that the goal, or focus, of the organizational change strategy must be related to the relative emphasis upon concept or experience. At the socio-organizational level a conceptual minimal threshold is almost certainly required before action research can successfully relate to organizational change.

8.3 Phases or cycles?

It is generally held that action research has a number of phases (see Section 12.1), but it is increasingly clear that any attempt to set down a number of phases is both likely to inhibit action research and to be inadequate as an account of what happens. We shall refer to elements which are likely to be found in action research, and we choose to emphasize cycles in order to avoid falling into the trap of following one or another of various competing phase models that exist. The case studies provide good evidence to show that such elements as problem definition, investigations, feedback, and design activities may all be occurring at approximately the same time. This point is heightened by the general opinion that in action research the practitioner must start creating the infrastructure to receive his diagnosis and solutions at the very start of the project. Hence we find this facility built into the formalized change programme of the Grid and introduced into my work at CCE.

The notion of cycles is strengthened by recognizing that there is, at most, a brief cycle of problem-definition, diagnosis, solution (PDS) and then a recycling. The whole process of practitioner and sponsor relations is characterized by both high interdependence and also considerable uncertainty, and recycling of the problem-diagnosis-solution has to occur in this context. In the case of the design of new hospitals and factories, the PDS cycle is complicated by difficulties of synchronizing all the various kinds of data and interpretation that are required. The complications of synchronization can be considerable, especially if (as in building and technological innovation) the concept of the end product has to be continually re-examined in the light of new information (see G. Higgin and N. Jessop, 1965; P. A. Clark, 1972, chap. 8). For analytical purposes we can identify the main elements as problem definition, diagnosis and solution.

In the first element, *problem definition*, the sponsoring system becomes aware that a problem may be resolvable by the application of the competences of behavioural scientists. Many accounts of organizational change indicate that sponsors are more aware of potential uses than practitioners (Lazarsfeld *et al.*, 1967; P. A. Clark, 1972; P. Hill, 1972) and this point is implicit in Greiner's schemata for successful organizational change (Section 21.1). However, these accounts also indicate that the sponsor is rarely able to articulate the key problem as defined by the practitioners, a point clearly illustrated in the O'Connell study. Problem recognition, and then contact with the practitioner, is one element which is seen as especially crucial in influencing the success of action research and organizational change. O'Connell and Greiner emphasize the significance of the initial situation and antecedent factors, but there are few studies, and even more surprisingly no comparative investigations, with, for example, the establishment of the brief in the relationship between architects and sponsors. We know from Jones that the sponsor's receptivity is particularly important in moulding the statement of the first definition of the problem and any subsequent modification. Once a definition has been agreed upon it influences the form and content of the change programme. This first element will include the practitioner's initial establishment of an internal system within the sponsor for receiving and diffusing later decisions. It will also include the practitioner's assessment of the sponsor's capability for managing the change.

In the second element, *diagnosis*, there is an extended analysis of the sponsoring system to establish the existing situation within the terms of reference specified by the accepted problem definition. Lawrence and Lorsch (1969) rightly comment on the casual nature of many approaches to diagnosis. In practice it should include both a mapping of the existing situation and the identification of the factors which are moulding, sustaining, and altering this situation. Diagnosis is utilized in two ways: it is both an account of what exists and why, and it also specifies in greater detail the most appropriate forms of solution. These points are summarized in my suggestion of the Alternatives and Differences Approach (ADA) which included selected feedback of the analysis and emerging solutions (see Section 4.4).

In the third element, *solution*, we include the evaluation of alternatives, the selection of the preferred solution and its installation (including modifications if required), and ending with the establishment of a new organizational state.

The major advantage of taking the PDS cycle and accepting that both recycling and a multiplicity of activities are occurring simultaneously is that this interpretation bears a closer resemblance to the actuality of action research. It is this actuality which we need to identify and utilize as the role model for the research approach to organizational change.

Summary

Intervention strategies, irrespective of other differences, are characterized by certain important common attributes in their approach to organizational change. They all make use of the concepts, variables and propositions from the behavioural sciences to diagnose and effect changes in some aspect of the sponsor's ongoing functioning. Also, they all tend to emphasize the importance of designing approaches that are systemic rather than individual. This is so for both the experiential and conceptual systemic approaches which are equally sceptical about the relevance of teaching methods utilized within the universities and colleges to transfer reflective knowledge for convincing the sponsor of the definition of problems, of the relevance of the diagnosis, and of the significance of the selected solution. I would argue that the conceptual approach gives greater recognition to importance of the diffusion of concepts in the sponsoring system.

The important differences lie in the extent to which strategies are directive or non-directive, an aspect of our earlier discussion of role models, and the nature of the emphasis upon experientially created data. In fact, it is the definition of *experientially* that is central because both systemic approaches seek to inject some concepts and both seek to convince by drawing upon the everyday experience of the sponsor as a starting point. However, those who emphasize the term experientially (or its generic title, the normative re-educative; see Chin and Benne, 1969) do this principally with reference to the people variable in the settings of small groups. This may be compared with my definition of the systemic conceptual, which is most relevantly applied to intervention strategies operating on all four of Leavitt's interacting variables. Here the practitioner does not draw upon the everyday experience of problem-solving styles within the group but recognizes that this might be a problem. Instead, and assuming that the group has some minimum problem-solving ability, he concentrates on the analysis of the organization as a whole in its balancing of the problem of internal management with external demands (see especially Parsons, Bales and Shils, 1953, chaps 3 and 5).

Although there does exist a controversy surrounding the generality of the experiential approach, I would suggest that we have placed the controversy in context by separating out the key dimensions of the level of unit which constitutes the sponsoring system and the range of variables considered relevant. For example, the experiential systemic approach is concerned with group performance in general terms with respect to problem solving without regard to the content of the problems. Its exponents contend that their work does lead to improved problem-solving ability, and the study at Sigma (Section 4.7) illustrates their case. The unit of analysis is the group and the range of variables is restricted to the people aspect. By comparison, I would suggest that improved problem-solving would not have helped either the insurance firm described by O'Connell or CCE to identify the kinds of problem tackled by the practitioners. In these cases the unit of analysis is the organization and the range of variables is for O'Connell the task and structure, and for CCE the entire range.

Given these differences in the nature of the units being analysed, the problems selected, and the focus adopted, then we may expect differences in intervention strategies. I would argue that both systemic approaches have much more in common than those who would dichotomise them would suggest. Both reject conventional academic teaching, but they do use the here-and-now in different ways. There seems to be very good reason why they should do so.*

* My analysis has side-stepped the conventional attack on the rational-empirical approach. This is explained in detail in Chin and Benne. My position as outlined above represents an analysis which can account for the case studies in a way which I feel Chin and Benne would find difficult.

CHAPTER 9

The organizational context of action research

In his examination of the uses of sociology, Lazarsfeld emphasizes that the relations between practitioners and sponsors, involving as they do a complex exchange of problems and knowledge, takes place in an administrative setting. The importance of the setting is recognized by all those who have argued that the sponsor's receptivity is more significant than any other aspect in influencing the outcomes of the research. In this chapter we shall examine the organizational context and administrative setting of action research with particular reference to the culture and structure of the organization.

We have now reached the point where it is necessary to give specific attention to the various ways in which this context constrains and facilitates the progress of attempts at planned organizational change. To achieve this requires some consideration of what we mean by organization. In this introduction we briefly consider the definition that has underpinned our analysis. A more extended discussion, set out in the following section, is of particular concern to students of organization. Some readers might prefer to jump to the exhibits and return to the section on organization at a later stage.

Can we assume that an organization is a closely interrelated system pivoted upon a well-defined and widely held set of values? Many of the strategies for applied and action research are based on this assumption. Hutte, in a subtle analysis of practitioner strategies and tactics, advises the practitioner to search out and work with 'the integer-power centres'. But the notion of an integer-power centre hardly applies in enterprises characterized by a multiplicity of decision-making centres in which co-ordination is achieved by bargaining within an arena of negotiation rather than by preprogramming. Given this diversity of structural forms, it is appropriate for action research to be organized to accommodate them, and we may anticipate that projects which do not will be unsuccessful. The significance of the examination of structural complexity and cultural diversity is illustrated by case studies from my own researches. The first explores the fate of a plant-wide incentive scheme over a period of some few years. The inability of the firm to control external events such as the price of raw materials contributed to the failure, but of equal relevance was the way in which the plan closely connected a number of independent and diverse production units with distinct structures and norms. The plan introduced tensions and altered the institutionalized network of conflicts, intensifying interdepartmental conflicts. The second case compares the development and acceptability of similar strategies of organizational design in two contrasting situations. This study is part of my comparative research on organizational change and the practitioner-sponsor relationship. The cases together show the importance of the antecedent situation and the structural complexity of organization, highlighting the practical problems of situations in which there are a plurality of decision-making centres.

9.1 Structural and cultural diversity

The concept of organization is central to the understanding of action research and of planned organizational change. The definition of organization most frequently adopted assumes that there is a single system of relationships which can be conceived in static terms. These assumptions are evident in the classic definition by Barnard (1938):

The special system of status associated with chains of command or hierarchy of authority depends upon each position being a 'communication centre', the inferior command being associated with restricted areas or fields, the higher command being more comprehensive.

We begin the examination of the concept of organization by adopting the distinction introduced by Blau and Scott (1961) between the system of social relationships and the cultural system. Its usage by Blau and Scott is reflected in their statement that the cultural system may be considered as a system of shared beliefs and orientations, which serve as standards for human conduct. But it is necessary to analytically separate the system of social relationships from the cultural system, for it cannot be presumed that a characterization of the social relationships will provide the basis for predicting the form and content of the cultural system. After making this distinction and observing the impossibility of predicting the form of one system from the other, we shall turn to a closer discussion of the cultural system, in which the thesis of shared values and beliefs is rejected as untenable and unnecessary. From this examination we shall construct a definition of organization that reflects current knowledge about behaviour in organizations. The definition will presume a multiplicity of systems and a dynamic situation in which the basis of the existing organization is always precarious and open to change (see Weick, 1970).

Traditionally, organizational analysts have adopted definitions of organization that assume a single system of relationships. Although such definitions have the advantage of facilitating certain forms of systems analysis, their development is of doubtful utility to practitioners (see Boguslaw, 1966) and to researchers (see Krupp, 1961). However, this type of definition is still widely recommended. Its adoption reflects the influence upon organizational analysis of theorizing derived from analogies developed in control engineering and biology, and it neglects the recognition of the distinctive features of sociocultural systems (see Allport, 1962; Buckley, 1967).

I would argue that 'organization' refers to a configuration of relationships and values, not to people, but there is some confusion about two facets of the interlocked behaviours (Weick, 1970) that constitute the relationships. First we may refer to social relationships, that is, to activities and interaction patterns. Their structure may be identified in a variety of ways, and there are already a number of techniques for achieving identification. Activities and interactions refer to the observable actions and contact patterns, including the frequency and duration of contacts, the patterns of initiation, and the directions of influence. There is a degree of overlap in this definition with the concept of 'task' as used by contingency theorists, and with the concept of 'constrained behaviour' suggested by Woodward (1970). In the original usage by Homans it is postulated that the activities in which a collection of people are engaged will influence the patterns of inter-actions, and there is some evidence to support this contention. For example, following studies of factory workers, Goldthorpe observes that there are features of the flow of work (activities) that facilitate or inhibit the frequency of interaction patterns (see Goldthorpe, 1967, Table 19).

In the original set of propositions suggested by Homans it is postulated that the greater the frequency of interaction the more likely are those involved to develop feelings of liking for one another. Thus

H

a predictive relationship between the systems of social relationships and the cultural system is implied. But it is possible to identify examples where increased interaction has led to greater hostility and conflict. Litwak observed that insufficient attention has been given by practitioners and researchers to the 'mechanics of segregation'. He points out that the bringing together of sub-units with differing objectives may increase the opportunity for conflict and exposure. Similarly, Van Doorn (1966) suggests that the lower the functional autonomy between sub-units the greater the likelihood of non-rational conflict. Etzioni, in a penetrating analysis of the division of compliance within organizations, makes a similar suggestion, indicating that the matching of boundaries between dissimilar units may be problematic for the relationships between and within them. When referring directly to this kind of situation, Merton (1957) uses the concept of role-set to discuss the problems that arise when the actions of members of the role-set become visible to one another. He points to the mechanisms that are developed to reduce visibility, and the implications of these for the persistence of the role-set. Collectively these observations do much to qualify the usefulness of Homans's proposition. It might be argued, however, that the practitioner requires a theoretical framework which focuses upon variables that are relevant to control and manipulation, and that the Homans framework provides this. Here we may note the observations of Emery on the practical problems in designing linkages between jobs which are interdependent. He suggests that the efficient operation of the task only requires that the members of the task group have sufficient mutual knowledge of each other's role to perform adequately. It is therefore unnecessary to postulate the requirement for friendship when mutual role knowledge is seen as crucial.

Another theory, known as 'technological determinism', ties social relationships to the cultural system. Exponents state that it is possible to determine the content of the cultural system from a profile of characteristics of the technology. A. Touraine has pointed out the limitations of this assertion.

We now turn to a closer discussion of the cultural system. It will be recalled that Blau and Scott emphasized shared beliefs and orientations. I should like to contrast this with the work of Bowers, who assumes the existence of interrelated groups, each within differentiated role networks, that share certain common objectives and possess some form of identifiable boundary. There are three ideas in this formulation which require discussion: (1) the concept of group;* (2) the concept of interrelationship; (3) shared objectives.

The concept of group. What characteristics of relationship are selected to identify a group? A tendency exists in some research traditions to presume that work groups in industrial settings are all typified by being highly cohesive and able to strongly influence the norms of what is a 'fair day's work'. In contrast, management frequently refers to a group of workers when in effect they mean an aggregate of persons who have been labelled similarly for the convenience of payment systems. In practice, the use of the concept of group by behavioural scientists is extremely loose. In comparative field studies T. Lupton clearly demonstrates the existence of both solidary and non-solidary work groups. His explanation of their existence focuses upon economic variables, especially the nature of labour and product markets (cf. J. W. Kuhn, 1961). We require a definition that takes account of the nature of values within the collectivity which is labelled group.

We cannot assume that the system of categories that management constructs for labelling aggregates 'jobs' provides an adequate insight into systems of relationships within a single enterprise. As W. H. Scott suggests, such a system of categories merely provides a starting point for analysis. Nor can we assume that the boundaries to collections of human tasks that engineers construct will necessarily also form the boundaries for the people who are employed in those tasks. It is, as Miller and Rice observe, essential to separate 'task boundaries' from 'sentient boundaries'. Sentient refers to feelings of involvement with a particular set of persons. Thus a first aim for the organizational analyst on change projects is to characterize the kinds of social grouping within an enterprise and to sketch out the most likely factors facilitating and inhibiting the continuance of the existing pattern (see P. A. Clark, 1972, chap. 7). An important development is the recognition that the motivation of men to join an organization is quite distinct from their participation in its activities once inside (March and Simon, 1958). Dubin has shown that work is not a central life-interest to many workers, and Schein has shown that the motivation of industrial man is best regarded as complex. In contrast, Bennis observes that many behavioural scientists assume that work is central in contemporary

* For a cogent and incisive examination of the uses and misuses of this concept, see R. T. Golembiewski, 1961.

society. That man is complex, that his interest in work is varied and variable, and that he is a member of a number of groupings must be taken into consideration when we think about planned change and its implementation.

✳ *The concept of interrelationship.* The nature of the connectiveness of groups can vary from close functional dependence to autonomy (Gouldner, 1959). This can best be illustrated by examining the idea of the 'front-line organization', which states that within certain enterprises there are sub-units in which the locus of initiative is situated with the persons supervising the units, the position of these persons is not open to either surveillance or easy assessment of the work done. For example, in the wards of the mental hospital one may find 'pockets of information' (McCleery, 1960) in which operating policy is effectively delegated to the 'front line'. Other examples of the front-line organization include the position of soldiers in combat as presented by Col. R. W. Little with reference to American soldiers in Korea. The value of the idea of the front-line organization is that it challenges the assumption pervading much of organization theory that the social and cultural systems are closely integrated.

The topic of the interrelationships between groupings and departments within organizations is increasingly recognized as an area for developing a social technology to improve organizational performance (as in the Managerial Grid). It represents an area in which the major part of organizational change strategies will be applied during the next decade. For this reason it is important that we do not overemphasize the benefits of integration of tasks and people. (An action research programme might advise that sub-units be separated.) Two European studies depict this aspect. Crozier's analysis of the interrelationships between management, female operatives, and maintenance workers in the French Tobacco Monopoly highlights both interdependence and conflict. It shows that the operatives have both the opportunity to undertake tasks which are the least predictable and also to do these in such a way that they constitute a key power group. Given that action research is inevitably involved in the political system of the organization (Long, 1962; Mechanic and Strauss, in Cooper *et al.*, 1964), then the understanding of power relations is central. Croziers' theory that those who occupy positions of uncertainty are in positions of power represents an important breakthrough. (The theoretical development of the analysis has been further advanced by Hickson *et al.*, 1970.) The second study is that by A. Flanders, in which he quite clearly reveals the delicate political manoeuvring between the parties involved during the introduction of productivity bargaining into the UK at the Fawley Plant of Esso.

✳ *Shared objectives.* Strong emphasis upon shared objectives is found in both theoretical work (e.g. Parsons, 1956) and in the working assumptions of practitioners. We have argued in the preceding sections that the assumption is neither theoretically or practically necessary. It can in fact prevent good research and interfere with applied work. Bowers, in a careful formulation of a definition of organization, suggests that we need only assume *some* shared objectives. This is sensible because it recognizes that the involvement of members in organizations might be quite low and this is not necessarily dysfunctional to the enterprise. Indeed it may be argued that industrial society rests on the premise that its members are able to cope with universalistic values rather than particularistic ones (Parsons, 1951). Many practitioners are concerned with providing a rationale for the working together of groups of persons on diverse tasks and the problems posed are neatly illustrated by the difficulties the 'cold war' concept posed for the transformation of the US military from a sole concern with battlefields to an involvement in the political life of the society. However, these problems cannot necessarily be solved by a crude belief in the culturally integrated organization.

The critics of Barnard's definitions of organization, with which we began our discussion, reject his assumption of a single, highly integrated set of interlocked behaviours, in a state of equilibrium, and strongly controlled by an integer-power centre. The defining features of sociocultural systems are their tendencies to create, elaborate and change their structure – that is, their morphogenic properties. There exist, both within and outside any particular enterprise, stable sets of alternative countervalues and an area of uninstitutionalized behaviour.* An adequate definition and analysis of organization requires the adoption of the 'process' model. This views social collectivities as a complex, multifaceted, fluid interplay of varying degrees and intensities

* Blau (1964) distinguishes the institutionalization of values and their legitimacy and gives prominence to imbalance and structural elaboration. His emphasis is upon the emergent properties of collectivities and upon the study of the actual associations between people. Although he does not examine how consensus authority can be legitimized, he does provide some insights into the 'frailty of authority' (Gluckman, 1959). Blau focuses upon the continual re-examination and re-definition of norms of fairness, and stresses the availability of alternative values.

of association and dissociation. An enterprise is seen as always changing its structure – for example, in exchange with the *perceived* environment. Hence the analyst must focus on the interaction of the elements in an ongoing system to reveal the differing degrees of structuring which develop, persist, dissolve or change. S. F. Nadel makes an insightful contribution to the non-static conception of organization by suggesting that the concept of structure is viewed merely as a heuristic tool. His focus is upon a structure of events. This valuable focus also characterizes the suggestions of F. Allport and S. T. Kimball. Kimball rightly emphasizes the neglect of the calendar of events within an organization. Nadel suggests that structure cannot be considered in the singular because 'there are always cleavages, dissociations, enclaves, so that any description alleged to present a single structure will, in fact, present only a fragmentary or one-sided picture'. This point is evident in Little's account of a combat unit in Korea and in my analysis of the effects of peak periods of working upon the management organization and intergroup relations.

This perspective on organization – the process approach – has a number of important implications for existing approaches to research on organizational behaviour and for action research. An obvious extrapolation is the contention that the study of attitudes at one given moment and without reference to the formative context is naive and simplistic.

Let us now consider some of the major factors influencing the form a particular organization takes. Contemporary theories emphasize two main sets of factors. First, the nature of the organizational task (e.g. Perrow), its environment (e.g. Lawrence and Lorsch), its technology (e.g. Woodward) and its rates of change (Burns and Stalker). Second, people and structures. The general tendency has been to under-emphasize the historical emergence of particular organizational forms (see Stinchcombe, in J.G. March, 1965), and yet this aspect is crucial for action research (see Greiner, 1967). In practice, the nature of the influences upon any single organization is a matter for on-the-spot inspection and investigation.

We have seen that the concept of organization is complex and that a wide variety of influences are significant in shaping a specific organization. It follows from this analysis, and especially from the process approach to organization, that the problems of actually creating and preventing changes are very great. To achieve directed, planned organizational change is incredibly difficult. This probably explains the broad generalizations that action researchers make about objectives, and is probably an important facet in Jones' discovery that whatever the objectives of published accounts of directed organizational change, there seem to be benefits!

If planned, directed organizational change is enormously hard to achieve, the explanation for the difficulty is fairly simple. There is no good reason to assume that the objectives stated by behavioural scientists are accepted by their sponsors. For example, when I attended my first T group I found it difficult to accept that its members' interests in learning more about group processes were as altruistic as the brochure suggested! It is apparent to a moderately astute person that insight into group dynamics can be used for a variety of individual ends. The same is also true of action research where the sponsors and subjects are not inert and passive. This understanding is central to analysing the role of the behavioural scientist in organizational change.

We summarize this section by stating that the process perspective on the definition of organization incorporates the major findings of contemporary researches and has the practical and theoretical usefulness of recognizing the complexity of the context in which action research occurs. A major strength is the rejection of the organization as a singular system of values operating through an integrated structural network. In place of this assumption the process perspective requires the analyst to investigate each enterprise as a stream of events that may or may not be incubating the seeds of unplanned organizational change. The analyst must assess the ways in which the process of the reaffirmation of the existing culture is taking place. Without this statement of the situation, any claims to be achieving planned organizational change may be taken as unproved.

In the sections which follow, the organizational perspective developed in this section is used to examine three examples of planned change so that the significance of the structural and cultural context of action research is highlighted.

9.2 A plant-wide incentive scheme (P. A. Clark)

Part of the work of the behavioural science practitioner should involve providing advice on the appropriateness of specific social inventions for the requirements of particular sponsors. In this kind of activity the practitioner must diagnose the characteristics of the invention and of the organizational context to which it is to be applied. This diagnosis is difficult because there is so little documentation of inventions and because there has been an unwillingness to apply the perspective of organizational analysis to the problems involved (Lippitt, 1965). Generally, sponsors prefer to see inventions as panaceas. In this section we examine the history of one invention, a plant-wide productivity scheme, to show how various factors influenced the 'failure' of the scheme in one firm in London.

Plant-wide incentive schemes received considerable support from D. McGregor. In one of the most influential books of the 1960s, *The Human Side of Enterprise*, McGregor argues that the capacity of individuals for intelligent self-control has been underestimated by executives when designing reward and punishment systems. The main thrust of his argument centres on the contention that if the members of an enterprise are provided with an organizational environment in which they are able to use their own capacities more fully than at present, they will accept the opportunity. McGregor believes that there will be an integration between the objectives of the individual pursuing self-control and the requirement by top executives for high performance.

The Scanlon Plan incentive scheme is an example of an invention designed to facilitate self-control and integration. Scanlon is said to have two desirable features. First, it is a device for sharing the gains from improvements in organizational performance among all those involved. It is not a conventional profit-sharing scheme, but rather it focuses upon cost reduction: the size of the payments are based upon the ratio of total manpower costs to sales. At the start of the scheme a ratio is agreed to, based upon past performance, and bonuses are paid monthly when the actual labour costs fall below the agreed ratio. This short time-scale provides rapid feedback on performance. Second, there is a formal provision for joint production committees that operate at all levels in the enterprise and may discuss all matters relating to production.

McGregor contends that the Scanlon plan does lead to arguments and heated discussion, but these are focused upon improved performance and are thus not divisive. However, he does observe that the learning period, when the plan is first introduced, can be tough. It might be argued that the plan is only appropriate in certain contexts. McGregor deals with three of the most frequently voiced objections and argues that size is not crucial and that he is optimistic about the variety of technological situations in which it may be applied.

The executive who is interested in applying Scanlon and similar schemes does not have a wide variety of sources of advice. Most of the accounts of success are very partial in their analysis, though there is no intent to deceive. Apart from an incisive comparative study by G. Strauss and L. R. Sayles – which was published in a journal not typically available to the executive – there is little systematic research.

When teaching in 1963 at a residential management centre specializing in short post-experience courses on the 'human aspects' for middle and senior managers, I considered the problems of application just as complex as the Strauss–Sayles study had hinted. Fortunately, a company in the London area had a plant-wide incentive scheme that was similar to Scanlon and they were willing to be a research site, so it was possible to make a retrospective reconstruction of the main events leading to the collapse of the plan.

Giles Products (pseudonym) is a long-established British manu- facturing firm with factories in London and the provinces. Its major production unit was at the London site, in an old area of the city. It consisted of three main factories employing 1850 production workers, 350 specialists and about 1300 staff. (This latter figure included members of the headquarters staff, e.g. sales.) The plant-wide incentive scheme was initially directed at the 1850 production workers, or more specifically, at about the 1400 who were not on piece work. The senior executives hoped that the scheme would replace piece work.

Though more than ten unions were represented on the site in 1958, there had been a long history of the settling of problems at the local level, and there was no evidence that the multiplicity of unions was in any way counterproductive. Senior union representatives had an influential position in the formation of policy for the operation of the plant, and the balance of union and management power was approxi- mately that suggested by Strauss and Sayles as favourable to a successful application. When the plan was introduced in 1958 the union repre- sentatives had full knowledge of the scheme and were agreed upon its desirability.

Figure 2 shows how the monthly bonus fluctuated during the four years in which the plan was in operation. At the start of the scheme the 22 per cent of the men on piece work, all members of supervision, store clerks and the 1300 headquarters staff were excluded. The bonuses were paid in pence per hour, and every worker included in the scheme received the same amount. This meant that the bonus had a higher impact on the pay packet of a young secretary than upon a highly skilled craftsman. In the trial period of three months small bonuses

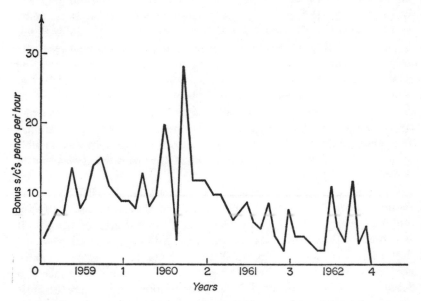

FIGURE 2 *Plant-wide incentive scheme: variations in size of bonus*
Based on H. J. Leavitt, 1964.

were paid, but when the scheme became established in the second half of the first year, the size of the bonus increased rapidly and complaints came from several groups who were not included. The supervisors complained, and after some bargaining received a special bonus payment. The store clerks complained because they had to work harder to calculate the stock figure which formed part of the means of calculating the bonus. The piece workers complained, and they were included later.

In the second year the bonus rose steadily, but in the third and fourth it began to drop, and by the end of the fourth year the scheme was in debt to the firm! During this period an increasing number of incidents occurred in which members of one sector of the factory blamed other sectors for not pulling their weight. Tensions increased. One union official commented that in four years the 'good will' built up over fifty years had been eroded. Moreover, not all the bonus problems occurred in the factory. The headquarters staff also pressed for an incentive scheme and were eventually successful. Unfortunately for them they joined too late and their special scheme was soon in debt!

We can see from Figure 2 how widely the bonus fluctuated from month to month. An analysis of the factors affecting the size of the bonus indicated that there were a number of influences over which the employees had no control. At one period the price of a major raw material fell while other factors stayed constant, and the bonus rose dramatically. Again, the actual composition of the 'sales mix' affected the bonus – some variations were caused by difficulties in stock-taking and accounting procedures. A senior executive reported that there was no good evidence to show that the size of bonuses was related to the activities of the joint committees established to manage production.

Earlier, reference was made to the existence of three separate factories. In fact, each of these was largely autonomous of the others in the workflow, and they had always operated independently without any demonstrable loss in performance. During the application of the bonus, conflict between the three factories increased and individuals found great difficulty in comprehending why the bonuses should vary so sharply. Subsequent discussion of the events indicated that there were a number of organizational features – all of which would probably have been salient to an organizational diagnosis – that made the incentive scheme seriously disrupt what Litwak has termed the mechanics of segregation. In effect, the bonus plan attempted to incorporate three semi-autonomous plants, each with distinct environments, technology and work force.

9.3 Organizational design in two contrasting enterprises (P. A. Clark)

We know that there is a wide variation in the extent and form of uses of behavioural science by enterprises, but we know little about the factors explaining this. For example, the extent of involvement by labour unions and religious bodies remains low when compared with industry and the military. Again, the nature of usage in the military seems to be very constricted and the possibilities for extending this are rather unpromising. It is not yet possible to demonstrate beyond doubt that the power structure of an enterprise influences the form of action research and the way it is used to achieve change.

Theoretically, the nature of the interdependencies between the sub-systems within a sponsoring enterprise would appear to be influential. A comparative study of the construction industry and mass production by Stinchcombe (1959) suggests that on theoretical grounds the infra-structures for receiving action research are very different in the two contexts. The comparison highlights differences in structure and co-ordination that are likely to influence the ways in which organizational change is achieved (see Section 2.2).

The question here is this: what is the fate of similar action research strategies in contrasting organizational contexts? In this case the approach that had been successfully applied in CCE Ltd formed the basis for action research of a similar team working in the British engineering industry. The setting of the second project was a production unit manufacturing a component of high quality for an engineering product of complex design. The international product market was highly competitive and subject to considerable turbulence and financial penalties. The prestigious parent company, Brit-Enj (pseudonym), which had many production units, was in the process of carrying through a major product innovation. At one production unit it had been decided to replace the existing factory with a new one that would be technologically superior.

The team commenced with a sociotechnical diagnosis to identify the key social–organizational differences between the existing and the planned factory. However, unlike the situation at CCE Ltd, this diagnostic survey met with considerable opposition and was the source of some concern for the senior managers who had persuaded the parent company that behavioural scientists could help to facilitate the transfer of personnel to the new factory. These managers were under some pressure, both locally and within the company, to justify the inclusion of behavioural scientists. The short-life project groups failed to get established, and our project coordinator began formal seminars as an alternative route to alerting the management to the kinds of problem he felt were important. For example, the local management suggested that there were few technological changes of magnitude, and that the consequences for their employees were comparatively small. The diagnosis, however, suggested more far-reaching changes in both aspects, but the kinds of feedback that succeeded in CCE Ltd failed here. The behavioural scientists therefore started a series of seminars, off the site, in which they presented the perspective of sociotechnical analysis, especially the work of the contingency theorists, illustrating the points from the diagnosis. This was designed to increase awareness. A tactic I introduced was to suggest to some of the managers in key positions that they should demonstrate the nature of the co-ordination system for the new factory by establishing a series of management games. This was selected to achieve the same objectives that had been reached using scenario writing in CCE Ltd. In some senses this was successful, and these alternative strategies created some greater cognitive similarity between our definition of the situation and the managers'; but there was no indication that this thinking was being translated into a program for action. After one year the program was terminated by the sponsor.

Although both the sponsor and the practitioner had believed that an action research project was desirable, they had differing conceptions of what it would contain. The sponsor constantly pressed for answers to problems which the practitioners did not feel had been established as problems. Essentially, the sponsor applied the purchase model to the relationship, and could not be shifted from that expectation to the dialogue, yet the characteristics of the problems selected required a relationship that would approximate the collaborative model. The social structure of the factory was more similar to the construction industry than to the mass production situation of CCE Ltd, and this suggested that the peritus approach would not necessarily be appropriate.

The emphasis by the sponsor on the short-time perspective and the delivery of answers, and the impossibility of altering this position holds several important lessons for action researchers. First, it is known (for example, from the work of Lawrence and Lorsch) that there are important differences in time perspective between managers from marketing, R & D, and production. At CCE Ltd, the key sponsors were associated with long-term planning and R & D, both of which typically adopt a long time-perspective and are used to dealing with the kinds of uncertainty involved in design work. Second, the sponsors at CCE Ltd were drawn from the men who were responsible for the whole company, and they were able to make decisions involving the allocation of time and money. Third, the areas of possible change which the CCE sponsors could initiate could be decided at their level, whereas in the second study the local managers' area of change was restricted by the need for comparability with other units in the same company and industry and by the requirements imposed by the organized craft groups. Fourth, there was a greater coincidence between the rational approach adopted by the consultants at CCE Ltd and their sponsors than between a similar team and their sponsors in the second project. That is not of course to suggest irrationality in the latter instance, but rather to point to the characteristics of decision making. These four differences illustrate the complexities of the context in which action research operates. Further investigation is required on the topic of matching types of action research to problems and to the sponsor's values and expectations.

It may be seen from the description of the second study in socio-technical design that the behavioural-scientist team was almost forced into the non-directive posture contained in the organizational learning approach of Revans. The problem was that of working through the implications of a diagnosis to a new action plan. This is certainly an area in which the practitioner has to be remarkably inventive – as the work of Paterson suggests – and it highlights the problems of achieving directed organizational change.

Summary

Our analysis of the concept of organization has shown the limitations of the single-system assumption. We have seen that organizations may contain highly differentiated cultures, work forces with complex and varying motivations, sub-units with varying degrees of functional inter-dependence. Given that organizations cannot be conceived of as single systems, we recognize that statements about systemic approaches to organizational change, and about types of organizational development which are confined to small groups of senior executives, must be re-examined. If a change programme is applied at only the top levels in an enterprise, then should we call this organizational development? I would argue that organizational design and change can only be accepted if they incorporate a variety of functions and a multiplicity of levels. For example, Paterson's activities included both the flying crews and the ground staff.

The consideration of the organizational culture and structure also assists the examination of the extent and timing of cognitive inputs (see Section 8.2). The strategy of organizational learning devised by Revans represents an intelligent matching of his preferred focus to the realities of the ideological concerns of those working in hospitals and to their complex power relations. In such a situation a non-directive emphasis has an obvious rationality. In contrast, Paterson was working in a crisis situation in a society that was at war. Here his covert expert role, a hidden peritus approach, is seen to be sensible. Hutte's concern for dealing with the key power centres in a public bureaucracy is also sensible. Again, the success of the organizational study by Clark and colleagues at CCE Ltd was strongly facilitated by the existence of the established design group, while the absence of such a group in the comparative study cited in this chapter seriously inhibited the adoption of a similar strategy, especially in a firm facing severe strains on resources.

In this chapter we have sought to demonstrate the importance of the organizational context in influencing the form and success of action research. We have emphasized the importance of the state of the sponsor at the start of a project, and the significance of matching the action research strategy to the value systems and structure of the organization.

CHAPTER 10

Focus, strategy and context

Those most heavily involved in the development of the uses of the behavioural sciences in organizations to achieve planned change have tended to place considerable weight on the importance of the relationship between themselves as practitioners and sponsors. They have stressed that sponsors as an audience are different from students. But are they right in emphasizing the collaborative relationship with sponsors? are they right in emphasizing experientially based strategies of the group-solving kind? are they right in giving cursory attention to the organizational context within which change is induced or directed, and within which action research has to occur?

From our introductory account of the varieties of research and approaches to organizational change, and from our case studies and their subsequent analysis, we can see that there are no simple answers to these questions. We have seen the considerable differences in role relations, the relative emphasis upon experience and concepts, and the contexts in which the practitioners and sponsor are operating. Are there any general patterns?

It is clear that the organizational context influences the possibilities for both change and action research. We know from the researches of Jones and others that the organizational and societal context are important. For example, it may be argued that Revans's approach, which is apparently disjointed and unintegrated, represents a well-judged intervention strategy for tackling on a large scale the problems of morale in institutions like hospitals, which are characterized by a professional and tri-partite authority system. His approach is designed to take account of the different frames of reference of the professionals working in hospitals. Again, it is clear that there are important differences in structure and culture (Section 9.1) between the military, with its secondary tasks and overlapping areas of work, residence and leisure, and industrial firms such as CCE. It is also clear that the sponsor's situation varies widely in the sense that some are facing actual crises (e.g. the insurance firm and Sigma), whilst others anticipate future problems (e.g. ICI and CCE).

116

In this chapter we examine the interrelationship between three aspects which we have thus far tackled separately. First, the topic of focus, by which we mean the practitioner's preferred point of intervention and problem territory. This may be one or more of the following: people, task, technology, structure (Section 3.1). Second, the topic of intervention strategy. Previously we have separated the role aspect and the intervention strategy to clarify the crucial points of the analysis, but these are now brought together. The intervention strategies may be viewed along two dimensions: the degree of relative influence between the practitioner and the sponsor on a continuum from unilateral to collaborative; and the relative emphasis in systemic approaches given to experiential data of the interpersonal type or of the whole enterprise interacting within its environment. Third, we have the context. This refers to the nature of the problem; the sponsor's situation with respect to crises; expectations of the practitioner; and control of resources. Also included under this heading is the practitioner's expectations.

The analysis in this chapter will be directed towards the identification of common patterns between focus, intervention strategy, and context.

10.1 The sponsor's situation and expectations

The existence of action research and the form that it takes cannot be explained solely by reference to the wishes, competence, and ideologies of practitioners. Their activities are financed by sponsors whose expectations and situation must be taken into account.

Tilles (1961), in an examination of the use of consultants by sponsors, provides an insight into the sponsor's side of the practitioner–sponsor relationship. He notes wide variations in sophistication amongst the sponsors using experts, and suggests that the crucial differences lie in the way sponsors think about the relationship. For example, a number of sponsors approach action research with the *purchase* model, which assumes that they are purchasing a product which the practitioner can supply. Implicitly it is presumed that the buyer can be specific, that both parties can establish conditions and a schedule for delivery, and that the price can be readily negotiated. Once the contract is signed, the sponsor continues as before and awaits delivery of the goods. It may be seen that the sponsor perceives the period between start and finish as the responsibility of the supplier and raises no questions about use. Tilles suggests that when a sponsor is seeking information, the

I

purchase model is appropriate. However, if the sponsor is seeking *help* rather than information – and this distinction is fundamental – then the purchase model is inadequate.

Another prevalent model favoured by sponsors is the *doctor–patient* relationship. Tilles humorously observes that the practitioner's preference for the term 'consultant' is perhaps not unrelated to the high prestige and fee-paying relationship associated with the term, but that it is misleading for several reasons: (1) Patients are usually ready to admit a problem, but few sponsors are prepared to say that the problem is 'with us'. Also, there is some obscuring, which we have already noted, of the size of the problem population. (2) The executive adopting this model absolves himself from being involved in the diagnosis. (3) It underplays the sponsor's shared role in the therapy. In action research the cure is rarely in a form comparable to the taking of pills, though some sponsors may attempt to obtain such a relationship.

Attention to the sponsor's favoured method of using outside resources is half of the total picture. The other half concerns the sponsor's actual situation with regard to a particular problem and his feelings of competence in handling the problem. For example, O'Connell states that in his study of the management consultant, the peritus role was expected by the insurance company and that it was the only way in which the sponsor's problems could have been resolved. O'Connell argues that given the specific goal, the urgency of the need felt by the client, the limitations of resources of finance and time, and the expectations of the sponsor, the change process could not have been achieved without the peritus role and the compliance intervention strategy. Hence it may be contended that the specificity of the problem definition, the sponsor's feelings about urgency, the resources of time and money available, and sponsors expectations all strongly influence the kind of approach adopted. O'Connell concludes by observing that practitioners have, in his judgement, given a low priority to the demands of time and the importance of economic criteria. Instead they have emphasized the social system, and have perhaps been reluctant to appreciate the leverage in organizational change that can be achieved by making alterations in technology, or in structure.

There are four main situational factors affecting sponsors which O'Connell selects and uses to demonstrate their influence upon practitioner and sponsor relationships. These are:

Factor	Scale
Specificity of problem and goal orientation	High – Low
Urgency of need by sponsor	Great – Slight
Availability of resources such as time and money	High – Low
Sponsor's feeling of competence at tackling the problem alone	High – Low

These four factors can be combined in various ways. If, for example, the problem is defined, the urgency great, resources scarce, and the sponsor expects decisiveness, then the profile will proximate to the peritus model. It must follow from this analysis that the practitioners who give emphasis to the collaborative relationship are most appropriately employed when the problem definition is diffuse, the urgency is moderate, the client has available resources and has relatively high feelings of competence.

10.2 Analysis of case studies

O'Connell's analysis may now be utilized to re-examine the connections between focus, intervention strategy, and context. For example, the collaborative model is undoubtedly strongly ascribed to by practitioners. It is evident in the organizational change work of E. Jaques (1951) at the Glacier factory and in the non-directive strategy of Revans. It may be postulated that these are all examples of action research with *broad aims*, sometimes representing a major innovation in the experience of the enterprise sponsoring the work.

The breadth of scope might explain the frequent reports of crisis or chaos at the start of a project. Jones reports that the typical action research programme starts with the practitioner taking the most initiatives and ends with his role being routinized (1969, Chap. 6). This observation, when coupled with O'Connell's analysis, introduces another possible explanation for crisis. It might be argued that practitioners have a tendency to perceive starting situations as crises, and that this is reciprocated in the sense that few sponsors have experience of using practitioners in broad aim programmes. In this explanation it is not necessary to postulate that the sponsor has low feelings of competence. For example, a comparison of the O'Connell study with the organizational design project at CCE would be as follows:

	O'Connell Study	CCE Ltd (Clark, 1971)
Specificity of goal	High	Low
Urgency of problem	Great	Medium
Resources available	Low	High
Sponsor's feelings of competence	Low	Quite high

At CCE the practitioner–sponsor relationship began in a collaborative dialogue *with important conflicts*, but gradually the initiative moved to the sponsor as the behavioural science input became routinized, hence the project followed the natural history suggested by Jones. We can now postulate that the explanation for the form of the project, the collaborative relationship, was strongly related to the diffuse nature of the goal, the sponsor's confidence in relating to the practitioners, the existence of spare resources to take part in the short-life project groups, and the long-term importance of the problem (construction of the new factory was some two years away at the start of the project).

An advantage of the analysis by O'Connell is the stress given to the interactive nature of relations between sponsors and practitioners. If we incorporate into our discussion the suggestion by Tilles that the sponsor's model of the appropriate relationship with the practitioner is the purchase model, then we have included a further factor that will influence the persistence and success of an action research project. For example, some members of the team who worked at CCE also undertook a somewhat similar organizational design project, but it was conducted under different conditions. A major British firm, Brit-Enj (pseudonym), was building a new production facility to cope with a recently acquired order for its products from a major American enterprise, and was experiencing the development stage of a product innovation at the same time that it was preparing for the new factory. Also, the development was being done against important financial penalties. In the second project (see Section 9.4) the organizational design was commenced after the major features of the technical design and plant layout had been established (cf. CCE), and at a time when there was increasing unrest at the key factory over both the product innovation and the move. Interestingly, the design of the new plant had been subcontracted (i.e. the purchase model) and there was no design group on site comparable to the Azimuth Group at CCE Ltd. The project began under some difficulties, as might be expected given the broad definition of the problem, but the sponsor began to request the expert model. This made the persistence of the collaborative relationship problematic. It might be argued that the nature of the problem was such that the peritus role would have been most appropriate, but this argument would underemphasize the difficulties of problem definition and the need for an interactive relationship in the early stages. The firm found it difficult to make resources available and did not have the same feelings of confidence about using practitioners as CCE Ltd. At the end of one year the project was terminated.

This example of organizational design, and its problems, lends support to O'Connell's assertion that to choose a role model and intervention strategy on a value premise is imprudent. The choice should be pragmatic. We may add that there are likely to be some situations where the possibilities for action research and organizational change are so poor that they should be avoided.

10.3 Appropriateness

Practitioner assumptions about focus typically include a set of beliefs about how that focus can be validated and made meaningful to the sponsor. We noted that in the early post-1945 days there was a strong movement away from intervention strategies that were based upon attempts to convince laymen by rational argument. Lewin's focus upon the people variable has been accepted by a high proportion of the practitioners in organizational development. However, it may be seen in Table 10.1 that, in fact, practitioners focus upon different combinations of Leavitt's four variables. At this point the key question centres on the linkage, if any, between action research as a strategy, the collaborative role, and the non-directive intervention strategy.

Given our definition of action research, and given that its exponents can draw upon all four of Leavitt's variables, they can in fact assess the adequacy of the schema to one crucial question concerning the appro-

TABLE 10.1   *Analysis of case studies*

SECTION	CASE	PROBLEM			SPONSOR			PRACTITIONER		
		Type	*Scope*	*Sponsor's confidence to tackle*	*State*	*Discretion*	*Resource control*	*Expectation of practitioner*	*Expectation of sponsor*	*Focus*
4.1	Hospital	Morale	Broad	Unknown	Normal	Medium	Medium	Experimental collaboration	Experimental collaboration	People
4.2	Insurance	Financial performance	Specific	Low	Crisis	Low	Low	Expert	Expert	Task, structure
4.3	Shipping	Technological change	Specific	Unknown	Existing problem	Unknown	Unknown	Social engineer	Collaboration with subject population	Social
4.4	CCE	Organizational design; new factory	Broad	High	Future problem	High	High	Collaboration and dialogue	Collaboration and dialogue	Technology, structure, people
4.5	Military	Accidents, morale	Broad	High	Crisis	Low	Low	Engineer	Covert expert in collaboration with subjects	Structure
4.6	ICI	Job design	Specific	High	Future problem	High	High	Employment of expert for demonstration study	Probably expert	Structure
4.7	Sigma	Market change and merger	Broad	Medium	Crisis	High	Probably high	Expert	Expert	People, structure
9.3	Brit-Enj	Organizational design: new factory	Broad	Medium	Existing problem, impending financial crisis	Medium	Low	Expert	Collaboration and dialogue	Technology, structure, people

122

priateness of collaborative and non-directive strategies rather than the other competing engineering and peritus models.

The engineering model may be eliminated because its exponents are *unlikely* to add to the stock of knowledge of the sponsor or to be able to contribute to organizational change. The remaining model is that of the peritus. Although the particular study by O'Connell was undertaken on a management scientist, this in no way undermines the relevance of the peritus role to behavioural scientists because it provides an opportunity to apply existing knowledge about organizational change and observe what happens. Thus we may conclude that both collaborative and peritus models facilitate action research, but the actual choice of model should be decided following a diagnosis of the sponsor's problem, role expectations and situation.

In the examination of the nature of action research, and of the appropriate form of focus and intervention strategy, there has been a gradual but discernible movement from a focus upon the practitioner to the organizational context of his activities. This shift in emphasis reflects an increased awareness that the existence and form of action research is strongly influenced by the sponsor's active demands, and by the structure and values of the organization. Thus C. Churchman and F. E. Emery (1967) stress the influence of the sponsor's value system, and Jones states that this variable is of greater significance than the practitioner's activities and competences.

The possibilities for action research are strongly, but not absolutely, influenced by the willingness of the sponsor to define the problem of organizational change in a spirit of inquiry. If the sponsor adopts this position then he is defining the stock of knowledge as something which can be changed, either by the verification of a hypothesis or by an imaginative innovation of a new paradigm, and it then becomes possible for both parties to work from a situation of consensus. Walton and McKersie (1965) refer to this state as integrative bargaining. However, if the sponsor assumes for whatever reason that the stock of knowledge is fixed, then exchanges are pivoted on its reallocation and the position is one of distributive bargaining. Integrative bargaining presents a situation for the practitioner in which there is an overt contract for action research, while the distributive bargaining position forces the practitioner to covertly undertake action research. This does not preclude action research, as the work of Paterson demonstrates, but it does introduce enormous additional practical problems.

Summary

In this chapter we have drawn together a number of important threads from previous analysis to suggest that the selection by practitioners of intervention strategies should be undertaken in terms of the focus selected and the state of the sponsoring system at the time of the organizational change programme. This conclusion challenges the established preferences and opens possibilities for a wider range of approaches to organizational change. However, our analysis has raised quite a number of problems for the action research approach to organizational change. We now turn to examine these.

CHAPTER 11

Privileged access

At all stages in our analysis we have emphasized the difficulties of achieving planned organizational change, and have pointed to the requirement to develop the uses of the behavioural sciences to a higher level of adequacy. I have argued that for learning about organizational change action research is one strategy that is particularly appropriate to gaining both more discriminated uses and more satisfactory long-term developments in theory and practice. However, it may be objected that there are a number of snags in the privileged access to the change process that make the appropriateness of action research doubtful. In this brief chapter I shall attempt to clarify the position of privileged access.

Let us begin by restating the definition of action research we have adopted: Action research is an activity that links the separate interests of scientists, practitioners, and sponsors; it tackles the theoretical questions arising in the basic discipline and multidisciplinary areas simultaneously with the practical problems of sponsors. Exponents of action research claim that they are able to achieve a privileged position within the milieu of organizational change, and that this position is frequently denied to many basic researchers in the pure basic and basic objective categories described in Chapter 2.

This claim has been challenged on several occasions, particularly in the overviews made of the activities of research agencies and similar institutions. Commentators have tended to be somewhat sceptical of the advantages of privileged access and typically have suggested that the action researchers neglect the power structure of the sponsoring system – in other words, that action research is making no noticeable contribution.

Critics of privileged access face a formidable task. For one thing, they have to offer a definition of action research that must as a logical minimum distinguish action research from other kinds of research; further, they must comprehend an activity that, as we have observed, exists at the moment only its early form: new, unroutinized, personalized, hidden. In effect, it may well be that criticisms arise from incorrectly labelling applied research as action research. The former does not claim, in our typology, to contribute to the solution of theoretical problems, although it may well be, as Cherns and Gouldner argue, that applied research is a fruitful source of ideas and illustrations for basic research. Also it is more than likely that a genuine mistake has arisen whereby actual examples of action research are misunderstood because the activities, interactions, and values that are most evident to the literature-based researcher do not conform to the idealized model of research purveyed in much of undergraduate teaching. The point is crucial because few academics have direct experience of action research, and indeed we have already noted a certain institutionalized tension between researchers and those associated with changing situations. The absence of direct experience means that the values of those involved in action research are inadequately understood.

Leaving aside the particular difficulty that critics face, it must be conceded that action research presents problems arising from the facing of two tasks, the theoretical and the practical, and three task masters – scientist, practitioners, and sponsors. It is clear that those who become involved must accept and work with a complex and changing division of labour, and here we start with an important feature of the research agencies that undertake action research. They are typically composed of people with both multiple interests and a multiplicity of interests, and it is through a balanced division of labour within such agencies that the major advances through action research to the study of organizational change are likely to occur. This is because a research agency can match a sponsor's problem with practitioners whose preference is towards problem solving and also with members who specialize in theoretical issues. Many existing research agencies, both independent and attached to universities, possess and are developing this characteristic. Thus it may be argued that the privileged position has not been inherently challenged, but rather its full potential has not yet been developed.

The failure to exploit privileged access when it has existed in the past may be attributed to the inappropriate model of the scientific process which has dominated research in the social and behavioural sciences during the past forty years. The behavioural sciences have become increasingly concerned with their professional status in relation to other already established scientific disciplines. Consequently they have emphasized that the behavioural sciences are in many respects like the natural sciences. It follows that the methods of investigating that are wrongly assumed to typify the natural sciences should be adopted. It was claimed that knowledge is unified, analytical, abstract and law-like – provided the theoretical frameworks could be sorted out. In this respect the similarities between Parsons and Homans in sociology are far more significant than the differences. In research there was a strong preference for the detached position and an increasing concern for the experimental situation (a good example is social psychology). This emphasis has become so firmly rooted that subjects like ergonomics – one most seriously permeated by natural science assumptions – have adopted the most simplistic conception imaginable of the laboratory experiment.

Experimental knowledge has until very recently been taken as a solid and dependable basis. It has been argued that situations are systematically constructed to explore and test hypotheses in ways that the field situation does not allow. However, a series of studies of the experimenter's role, the behaviour of subjects in the experimental situation, and the position of the research assistant has revealed a crisis of confidence in the experimental strategy as originally conceived.*

The practical difficulties of having a research role in a change situation are superbly illustrated in the interesting analysis by Gross and colleagues (1971, pp. 41 ff.) of the failure of an educational innovation known as the catalytic role model. Here the researchers attempted to place an independent researcher in a change situation involving a small number of teachers in one school. These teachers found the innovation very difficult to comprehend, and it is reasonable to assume that they were equally commonsensical about the main researcher who proceeded with the conventional approach of the detached, ever present observer. Indeed, this study (unfortunately) provides a fair illustration of the mechanistic approach to intervention so neatly depicted and so sharply appraised by Argyris in his examination (1971, chap. 4) of the unintended consequences of rigourous research.

My aim here is merely to point to some of the limitations of established notions of the scientific sanctity of experimental approaches as currently practised, not to propose their abandonment. These established

* The collection of essays by W. M. Evan, 1971, provides an excellent overview of the main viewpoints. See especially Part III and contrast S. E. Seashore with L. B. Barnes.

approaches are utilized by their exponents in a way that is frequently quite innocent of the social structural characteristics of the context in which they are applied. But it is one thing to devise an experimental design for comparing the growth rate and performance of seeds, and quite another to apply the same design in its entirety to the study of people (see L. B. Barnes, 1967). Gouldner rightly suggests that there should be an increasing self-consciousness amongst behavioural scientists and he proposes a reflexive sociology. Similarly, I would argue that the researcher should build an awareness of how other actors interpret his role into the interpretation of the situation (Cicourel, 1964). An advantage of the privileged access arising from the helping role is that it is a meaningful role to the sponsors, who are also, from the action researcher's viewpoint, subjects.

To summarize: the value of privileged access is implicitly recognized in the more general use of participant observation. In effect, there is very little participant observation of managerial decision-making because researchers are rarely also credible managers outside the universities and research institutes. However, the role of the problem-oriented researcher is recognized and it does provide, because of the privileged access, an especially interesting opportunity to develop theory and practice. This is not to say that no difficulties exist, but rather to argue that they have been exaggerated by simplifying the advantages of conventional approaches.

CHAPTER 12

Models of knowledge utilization

To use behavioural science perspectives within enterprises to achieve organizational change requires the development and integration of models of knowledge utilization that will connect the sponsoring enterprise with the full network of institutions concerned in the generation and application of knowledge. Dissemination and utilization cannot be understood without reference to society as a whole and the major systems involved in the generation, production, distribution, and consumption of knowledge. Similarly, problem solving and the development of social inventions cannot proceed satisfactorily in isolation from the sponsor's general state of awareness.

In this chapter we shall move to a wider view in order to discuss the topic of knowledge utilization as a whole.*

The universities are one of the primary sources of knowledge. They store knowledge and are cultural carriers of expert knowledge (Etzioni, 1961), but do not take responsibility for dissemination and use. These functions are performed by the professions, and by product and service organizations (e.g. market intelligence agencies). The consumer's power to influence the role of the universities is in many ways very limited, though indirect influence is the subject of considerable social and political controversy, as recent events in universities around the world have shown. Within the universities and professions, the research world specializes in the production, certification, and storage of general knowledge. The universities are second only to the government in being the chief servant of society. Although the universities have a great problem-solving potential, it is rarely used, and in many ways the universities are a prison for new ideas and hardly ever initiate co-ordinated interdisciplinary activity. In effect, the universities are ambivalent about their role in problem-solving. In contrast to the world of research, those involved in the practice of behavioural science

---

* This chapter draws on the work of Havelock *et al.*, 1969, *Planning for Innovation Through the Dissemination and Utilization of Knowledge*, Ann Arbor, Mich.: Institute of Social Research, University of Michigan.

work in three crucial interfaces: with researchers, with sponsors who purchase their assistance, and with other professionals (against a tradition of professional rivalry). The practitioners operate in a milieux in which few sponsors have developed skill at 'knowledge utilization'.

The utilization of knowledge has two main facets. First, there is knowledge building, that is, the integrating of relevant research and theory into forms that can be utilized outside the immediate scientific community. The increase in the number of social inventions bears witness to the increasing relevance of this development work – examples include the Managerial Grid, System 4 Management, the autonomous group, and job enrichment. The second aspect is the institutionalizing of knowledge, that is, the creating of networks and pathways for knowledge to be introduced into consumer organizations and then acted upon.

Much of our own discussion of the practitioner–sponsor relationship has been dependent upon the dissemination of ideas through journalism, seminars, and short courses. In this chapter we examine three major models of the process of dissemination and utilization with reference to organizational change. The *problem solving model* focuses upon whether change is required, which directions it should take, and what means should be used. The strength of the problem solving model is its focus upon the internal state of the organization; its weaknesses lie in the neglect of the wider situation. The wider context is dealt with in two contemporary models, the diffusion model and the research–development–diffusion–adoption model, which are also examined in this chapter.

12.1 Problem solving model

Lewin, who was particularly interested in the research and action approach, may be regarded as one of its early supporters and exponents. He advocated a closer interdependence between research, training, and action. This led to his support for action research as a strategy for change, and for the participative method in groups as a medium of re-education. In this approach, later described by Chin and Benne (1969) as the normative and re-educative approach, the clarification and reconstruction of values is of pivotal importance to obtaining organizational change. The chosen method seeks to get the sponsor's values out into the open arena for examination and self-discussion. Lewin recognized that in his formulation of action research the roles of the subject and the practitioner are sometimes switched: the subjects become researchers (as on the project in the ten London hospitals – see Section 4.1), and the researchers become men of action. This switching of roles is designed to facilitate unfreezing.

Lewin saw behaviour as a dynamic balance of forces working in opposite directions within the sociopsychological space of the enterprise. In the Paterson study of flying accidents, his theory would postulate a balance between the forces generated by the ground types, especially the commanding officer towards reducing accidents, and the desires of the frustrated pilots to demonstrate their excellence. The formal methods of change attempted by the commanding officer and the training device introduced by Paterson did nothing to alter this balance of opposing forces. It was only when Paterson reconceptualized the problem and became an active agent in clarifying and reconstructing values through working on the social structure of the airfield that the balance became disturbed and change was possible. In Lewin's conception there are three phases to organizational change:*

1. Unfreezing of the existing dynamic balance of forces
2. Moving to a new position
3. Refreezing at the new position

Within the unfreezing stage we should include both the development and articulation of the need for change (i.e. problem definition) and the establishment of the change relationship between the sponsor and the practitioner (Lippitt *et al.*, 1958). The practitioner is aiming to stimulate a desire for improvement. For example, the early phases of the application of the Managerial Grid as presented by Blake and Mouton elicit – from members of the sponsoring enterprise – definitions of the existing levels of performance and the desired levels of performance. A simple comparison of these two provides specific goals for the grid programme.

Recently, Schein has attempted to conceptualize the unfreezing process more precisely by drawing on Goffman's analysis of 'face work' (see Bowers, 1970). Schein suggests that there are three features of

---

* This simple formulation has been enormously influential in the discussion of directed organizational change. It is still explicitly recognized in the revised chapter, 'Change Stretegies', in the latest edition of Bennis *et al.* (1969), but is questioned by Froehman (1970).

the social perceptions of reality by sponsors which are important to unfreezing:

1. Self image
2. Definition of the situation
3. Image of others

Schein contends that the disconformation of one or more of these can be the basis for unfreezing. For example, in my study of organizational design, the sponsors were presented with an analysis of their own designs for the future which indicated that these would eliminate certain features which they wished to see introduced and incorporated.

Lewin's conception of unfreezing, and his three-phase model, underly the extensive examination of the planning of change by Lippitt *et al.* Their analysis focuses upon the practitioner–sponsor relationship, postulating the following stages:

1. Development of a need for change
2. Establishment of a change relationship
3. Clarification or diagnosis of the sponsor's problem
4. Examination of alternative routes and goals; establishing goals and intention for future action
5. Transformation of intentions into actual change practices
6. Generalization and stabilization of change
7. Achieving a terminal relationship

This extended formulation may also be found in the eight-phase model suggested by the National Training Laboratory in 1966, and in the nine-phase model of Buchanan (1967) devised for practice in the educational system of the United States. The latter two place rather more emphasis upon the requirement for assessing both the capabilities of the practitioner to solve the problem and the potential of the sponsor for establishing a viable relationship.

The main features of the problem solving model are set out in Figure 3.

Antecedent factors – which Greiner suggests are vital to the success of action research – are dealt with explicitly by Gross, Giacquinta and Bernstein (1971) following an attempt to implement a major educational innovation. The increasing reference to antecedent factors in the phase-models by later writers and practitioners suggests that the followers of Lewin who attributed non-success to resistance to change may have taken too restrictive a view of the complexities of the process.

The seven-phase model of Lippitt, with allowance made for an extended analysis of antecedent factors facilitating and inhibiting the potential for organizational change, provides one of the most useful formulations. For example, the Paterson analysis of the group processes on the air field as a prerequisite to change emphasizes the importance of stage 5 – the transformation of intentions into actual change practices.

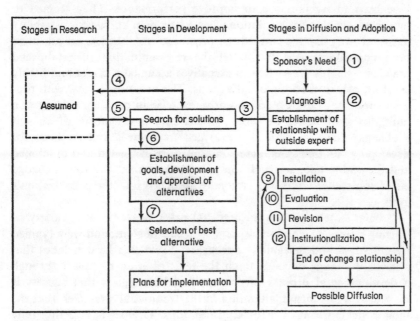

FIGURE 3 *Problem solving model*
Based on R. G. Havelock *et al.*, 1969.

Lippitt's model has strong similarities to the findings of Greiner (1967) who is one of a small number of researchers who have attempted to identify the phases of successful change programmes.

Greiner focused upon the following aspects in the selected sample of 18 studies:

– Conditions leading up to the attempted change

K

- Manner in which the change was introduced
- Blocks and facilitators encountered during implementation
- Results that appeared over a period of time and were more or less
  lasting

The application of these categories was somewhat difficult because not all the studies selected contained the necessary basic information. However, it was possible to detect a general pattern in the successful cases. Typically, in the successes, the top management had for some time been under pressure to improve performance. They seemed to have been groping for a solution when a new man known for capability in introducing change entered the organization (either as an executive or a consultant) and facilitated the re-examination of established practices. At this stage the top executives assumed a direct and highly involved role in carrying out diagnosis. The new man – now with top-level support – began a collaborative exercise in problem solving at a multiplicity of levels in order to facilitate a diagnosis of current problems. The new man also provided fresh ideas and methods for developing solutions. As these solutions were evaluated and developed and the viable ones selected, the general movement towards a change effort commenced and was gradually absorbed into the organization's every-day life.

Greiner notes that the unsuccessful cases began from a variety of starting points, had an inconsistent sequence of steps, and were typified by unilateral and delegated approaches. From this he concludes that successful change depends upon the redistribution of power through a developmental process of change, and he suggests that success is related to a significant alteration in the traditional practices that the 'power structure' uses in making decisions. Greiner is referring only to the process of changing from one state to another, and thus is not necessarily implying that shared power will continue once the new state is attained. The observations concerning the *developmental process of change* are important for understanding the limitations of evaluations of action research outlined in Chapter 2. In part, Greiner's thesis is somewhat negative: 'Organizational change is not a black to white affair occurring overnight through a single causal mechanism'. He does develop his case more convincingly when arguing that organizational change contains a number of phases, each holding specific elements and multiple causes, which in turn elicit an interpretation and response from the established 'power structure' which itself sets the stage for the next phase.

Greiner's proposed model of the dynamics of successful organizational change contains six phases, each of which starts with a stimulus being experienced by the established power structure (the dominant coalition), which is the source of a response that leads into the stimulus for the next phase:

1. Pressure on top management, which leads to the response of a determination to take action
2. Top-level intervention and the general response of a reorientation to internal problems
3. Diagnosis of the problems and the recognition of specific problems
4. Invention of new solutions which elicit commitment to new courses of action
5. New action plans resulting in experiments with selected solutions, these in turn provoking a search for results
6. Reinforcement from positive outcomes and the eventual acceptance of new practices

The main strengths of this six-phase model are that it takes account of the context of the sponsoring enterprise and the internal power structure, that it depicts change as a process, and that it emphasizes the working through of change proposals. Greiner seems not to have taken into account the excellent study of 'working through' by Flanders (1964) in the analysis of the Fawley productivity bargain at Esso, and thus underplays the interactions between the sponsoring groups and other groups in the development of change (see Chapter 9). But Greiner's analysis does much to clarify the importance of the temporal sequence of events in influencing the successful outcome of action research programmes, and it recognizes the important roles of the key sponsoring groups and the practitioner, although it excludes the kinds of expectations each might have. The six phases illustrate the problems facing the researcher seeking to investigate attempts at directed organizational change, and the difficulties of conceiving of change as a single event. The phases do, however, contain several distinct processes which may be analytically separated to some advantage.

Dalton (1970), in a keynote paper summarizing much of his own and previous research, suggests that there are four important sub-processes. The first concerns the setting of objectives. It is argued that in successful change there is a movement from generalized goals to specific objectives, during which the practitioner is especially influential with the sponsor, to a more ordered state in which the role of the practitioner is routinized and influence is reduced. (A similar point was made by Jones.) The second sub-process concerns the erosion of established sociopsychological ties built around ongoing behaviour patterns, and their replacement by new relationships. Third, there is the transformation of the sponsor from a state of self-doubt and lowered personal judgement to one of heightened feelings of competence to tackle problems (as O'Connell). Fourth, there is the change from an externally experienced pressure for change to an internalized motivation for success.

The major strength of the problem solving model is the focus upon events within the sponsoring enterprise and its enacted environment. The limitation is that it cannot explain how the sponsors became aware of and interested in using action research to effect organizational change.

12.2 Diffusion model

The basic unit of analysis in the diffusion model perspective is the individual, and the focus is upon the individual's perception of and response to external knowledge. This might be the diffusion of knowledge about new drugs or new medical practices (see Coleman, Katz and Menzel, 1966). The model attempts to establish the stages through which an individual must have passed before adopting or rejecting a new social practice. An important feature of the principal model, developed by Rogers and set out in Figure 4, is that it assumes the existence of the practice and is therefore not concerned with either research or development work in creating the practice. There are five main stages in the model suggested by Rogers:

1. *Awareness.* An individual is aware of a new invention, but is not necessarily motivated to learn more about the details or consider adoption. Awareness may not be related to need (cf. the crisis hypothesis), but may lead to the development of a need. Essentially this is a passive stage for the individual.
2. *Interest.* The individual actively seeks for information but has not yet judged its utility. (Rogers emphasizes here the role of personality and social-system variables in influencing the search process.

3. *Evaluation.* The individual mentally relates the new invention to his present and future states, and decides whether to experiment with it.
4. *Trial.* This only occurs if the mental trial (evaluation stage) suggests advantages to the individual. Typically, the innovation is applied on a smaller scale in order to determine its utility to a particular situation.
5. *Adoption or rejection.* Adoption occurs if the results of the trial are judged favourably.

We may illustrate the model by taking one of the case studies cited in Chapter 4: job enrichment. The research conducted in ICI by Paul,

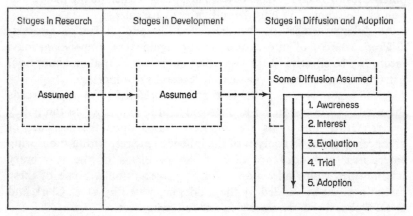

FIGURE 4
Based on R. G. Havelock *et al.*, 1969.

Herzberg and Robertson represents the trial phase, and its successful outcome influenced others within the firm to adopt the innovation. This example implies that certain catalysts and pacemakers had become aware of and interested in the general ideas of motivation associated with the names of McGregor and Herzberg and had decided that they were of relevance. The significant feature of the job enrichment experiments cited by Paul and colleagues is that the innovation had a number of features which made it possible to apply it on a trial basis and evaluate the results without disrupting the whole firm. This facet is somewhat neglected in Rogers's formulation, although he emphasizes the characteristics of successful innovations:

– relative advantage to sponsor
– compatibility with the existing system
– low complexity relative to sponsor's experience
– divisibility into elements that can be experimented with
– ease of communicating results

The general model of Rogers has been influential among those adopting the diffusion model, and it is widely accepted in its full form.* One important variation has been introduced by Holmberg, who places trial before evaluation. Also, some models emphasize a stage prior to awareness in which there is a consideration of the awareness of practices; others add a stage beyond adoption to include the incorporation of the innovation into the individual's routines.

At different stages in the dissemination and utilization process, different sources of information are of significance. Impersonal mass media can be effective at the awareness stage, but at trial and adoption, personal communication (i.e. action research) is important.

A limitation of the model is that it is oriented primarily towards the needs of the researcher and provides little assistance to the policy maker. Other limitations are that it is based upon the existence of practices, neglects an analysis of the influence process within sponsoring enterprises, and does not discuss the problems of the temporary relationships which all action research projects imply. Some of these limitations can be tackled by the model suggested by D. L. Clark and E. G. Guba, which we discuss in the following section.

12.3   Research – development – diffusion – adoption model (RDDA)

Generally speaking, the RDDA approach, set out in Figure 5, suggests an orderly process commencing with the identification of a problem, followed by activities to discover a solution, and ending with the diffusion of the solution to a target population. The perspective starts earlier than in the model of Rogers, hence it includes a more complex array of roles and network of relationships. The major developments of the model have come from work in the field of education. This fact is just as important as the influence on the Rogers formulation of the problems of studying isolated decision makers such as doctors

---

* See J. Langrish *et al.*, 1972, *Wealth from Knowledge: A Study of Innovation in Industry*, London: Macmillan.

and farmers. Indeed, the influence of the organization of the educational system upon the RDDA perspective cannot be underplayed. We have selected the work of D. L. Clark and E. G. Guba because it complements that of Rogers by giving greater attention to the theory-practice continuum.

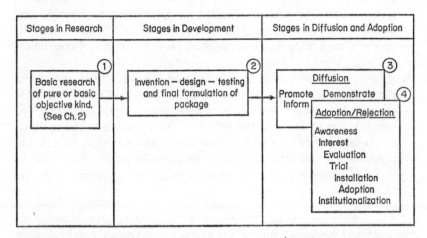

FIGURE 5

Based on R. G. Havelock *et al.*, 1969.

In practice this model does tend to suggest a left-right movement for applied work from theory to application. This notion has been challenged in the studies of innovation by Carter and Williams, by the model of applied work formulated by the Tavistock Institute (1964), and by Cherns's analysis of models for the use of research (1972). However, allowing for this limitation, the model presented by E. G. Guba does have a number of useful features:

1. *Research*. Research is undertaken to advance or extend knowledge. It can be evaluated only in terms of its own validity, not whether it leads to innovation and change (cf. the arguments advanced in Chapter 2).
2. *Development*. Development includes invention and design. The objective of invention is to formulate a new solution to a class of operating problems. In practice this may be based upon research, experience or even intuition. It is evaluated in terms of appropriate-

ness, viability and potential significance. The object of design is to order and to systematize the components of the invented solution into an innovation package suitable for institutional use. Evaluation of design is in terms of feasibility, performance and generatability.

3. *Diffusion*. The invention or design is disseminated to create awareness and is evaluated in terms of the message. This is followed by a demonstration, or trial, to afford an opportunity to examine and assess the operating qualities of the invention. Evaluation is in terms of credibility and convenience, plus the degree of conviction which its assessment of evidence provides.

4. *Adoption*. The invention is incorporated into the client system via three main activities: (1) The trial, to provide familiarity. It is evaluated in terms of performance and adaptability. (2) Installation, which is concerned with the fitting of the invention to the context. It is evaluated in terms of effectiveness and efficiency. (3) Institutionalization; the invention must be assimilated. Evaluation is in terms of continuity and the support given to the invention by the local sitting.

The formulation of Clark and Guba is designed to give attention to the relatively neglected topic of the gap between research and practice; it represents an attempt to bridge that gap. In the past, they state, insufficient attention was given to the planning and co-ordination of knowledge dissemination and utilization.

Clark and Guba do not expect the stages to appear in every situation; the aim of their model is to provide both the practitioner and the sponsor of action research with a framework for organizing their observations. In that sense, the model is angled to the requirements of the practical situation, and its authors observe that the four-stage process can break down at any point.

In general, the models in the RDDA category are more variable than in the diffusion approach. For example, the model developed by Havelock and Benne (1969) from their studies in the American Telephone and Telegraph Company was formulated in a context that was highly structured and integrated, even when compared with the context in which Clark and Guba were working. Obviously, there are significant differences between the organizational context of AT & T and the educational system, hence it is not surprising that Havelock finds a pre-existing division of labour and an elaborate linkage network which Clark and Guba did not find in education. This suggests that the distinction between the research phase and the development phase will be sharper in AT&T.

Before leaving these models, let us briefly consider one important point arising from the work of Bricknell (1966). Bricknell studied an instructional innovation in the New York State school system that required considerable structural rearrangements. In that context, he observed that three phases – design, evaluation and dissemination – are distinctly different, irreconcileable processes. This observation again emphasizes the problems that face evaluation researchers who seek to assess the performance of broad action programmes.

12.4 The role of research institutes and foundations

In this chapter we have examined a number of models that highlight the main phases in the organizational change process. These models presumed that the sponsor was aware of, and interested in, the behavioural sciences and action research. In contrast, the models of Rogers and of Clark and Guba largely neglect the situation within the sponsoring organization.

The diffusion model of Rogers tends to assume the prior existence of a social practice and to focus attention upon the speed with which a particular practice flows through to potential users. A strength of this approach is the examination of the whole network of social relationships, and particularly the position of users within that network. It is, however, sketchy on the psychological processes and surprisingly neglectful of the vast and important literature on behaviour in organizations. This limitation is in part balanced out by the concentration upon the delineation of informal relationships and upon reference groups, and the awareness that different kinds of influence strategy are required at different phases in the process. The RDDA model of Clark and Guba does tend to assume a rational sequence of events, though its advocates do not assume that knowledge flows in a linear pattern. *Recycling*, as a constant feature of design and redesign, is explicitly incorporated into the model. The model is excessively oriented towards the needs of the researcher. It either neglects the user or presumes that he will occupy a passive role. We know from the case studies in Chapter 4 and the analysis of the relations between behavioural scientists and their employers that this assumption over-simplifies the problems of undertaking action research.

The three types of model are most useful when viewed collectively as a source of insights and guideposts to understanding and planning the utilization of knowledge. The importance of integrating the three models may be seen by examining the role of research institutes, agencies and foundations. Many of the examples cited in this and the earlier chapters are drawn from the activities of research institutes of various kinds – The Center for Organizational Studies at the University of California, Los Angeles; the Work Research Institute, Oslo; The Center for Applied Social Research, Columbia University; the Tavistock Institute of Human Relations, London; the Institute of Social Research, Michigan. Such institutes make important contributions to the dissemination and utilization of social research, to the practice of action research, and to the development of a cross-disciplinary knowledge about specific problems in organizational change and innovation. Frequently, their activities are just as much misunderstood as is action research – typically, they are accused of not conforming to the accepted pattern of pure basic research as set out in my typology (Section 2.1). Consequently, the exact nature of the contribution of problem-oriented research institutes is obscured, and successive generations of students are treated to apparently scholarly critiques of the limitations of their theoretical basis and status.

One of the best known research institutes in Europe is the Tavistock Institute of Human Relations. Members have played a central part in developing action research as a methodology (see Foster, 1971) and in directing attention to the design of systems of organization in all kinds of enterprises (e.g. ships, prisons, hospitals, education) and the family (e.g. the social basis of mental illness). One of the best-known overviews of their activities in the industrial field is the careful assessment by R. K. Brown (1967) of Tavistock's contribution to the subject area of industrial sociology. The overview shows some of the problems facing members of the sociological community in locating applied work within any relevant theoretical scheme, not least because of Brown's assumptions about the objectives of Tavistock's researches. I would argue that industrial sociology in the United Kingdom began by including the activities of action researchers and applied researchers as well as bits of numerous other disciplines, but that it would be quite wrong to claim that members of the Tavistock see their principal aim as developing industrial sociology. Indeed, Brown cites no convincing evidence to show that this is the case. Thus the implied criticism of the Tavistock members for confusing consultancy and research is misplaced because their contribution is principally to the development of a professional knowledge and applied practice about problems. I would contend that the correct posture for the sociologist would follow more closely the analysis of the role of behavioural scientists in relation to industrial enterprises and organizational ideologies as initiated by Bendix and developed by J. Child.

An alternative, and I feel a more fruitful, approach to the examination of the role of research institutes and foundations in knowledge utilization is suggested by B. Harris in an analysis of the part played by the Nuffield Foundation in facilitating curriculum reform within the educational system of the United Kingdom. He uses a Parsonian perspective to examine the sources of stability within the educational system that inhibited innovation and curriculum change. The principal structural inhibitions to change may be identified as the schools inspectorate and the examination boards, and the main cultural factor of significance may be identified as the social value of autonomy for the teachers and the school. Given these structural and cultural factors, how could change occur? Harris sensibly argues that a Parsonian perspective is best treated as a logical construction in which system stability and change within its framework can be fruitfully examined. The role of the Nuffield Foundation was crucial in the early phase of innovation, when funds from the Foundation facilitated the creation and establishment of interest groups incorporating teachers and external agencies who carried out experiments in particular settings. (This may be compared with the work of Paul and colleagues in ICI.) Thus external agencies, including representatives from the universities and from industry, linked with teachers sympathetic to change in a way that made use of the structural factors of the English educational system and did not directly and overtly infringe upon the notions of autonomy so central in the value system of the teaching profession. These small experimental groups were mobilized and sustained by resources of finance and legitimacy from the Foundation. The groups then provided the crucial connection in the diffusion chain, linking teachers with other external agencies. Change was introduced through experiments without overt centralized control. The operating method of these innovative groups incorporated important elements of both the rational-empirical approach and the normative-educative approach and thus illustrated the value of not separating these for simply ideological reasons (cf. Bennis, Benne and Chin, 1961). The analysis by Harris complements the emphasis of American educationalists upon the research-application linkages, and points to the importance of integrating the three main models of knowledge utilization and creation.

Summary

Clearly, the existence of action research is highly dependent upon the diffusion throughout society of an awareness of and interest in the behavioural sciences and the action research strategy. This process gathered momentum throughout the 1960s in Europe, the United States and Australasia. But diffusion is insufficient. The strength of the problem solving perspective is that it points to the importance of the situation within any organization for facilitating the actual *existence* of action research, and to the influence that the organizational context has upon the form of the relationship and the kinds of knowledge utilization. Both these perspectives are valuable, but their utility is strengthened by incorporating the ideas developed by Clark and Guba for linking research with development through to application. The significance of this is evident in the problems of organizational change within such institutional complexes as educational systems and also in understanding the emergence and application of particular social practices like the managerial grid and organizational development.

Finally, we have pointed to the importance of the research institutes and foundations. The study of the role of the Nuffield Foundation by Harris indicates the crucial part such bodies can play in innovation and organizational change. In the particular case we have examined, the Foundation limited its activities to an entrepreneurial role and gradually moved away from the scene as curriculum reform became institutionalized. The role of other institutes and funding bodies has been rather different. The Office of Naval Research in the United States has played a significant role in supporting problem-oriented research (e.g. on leadership styles) and in dissemination and the Tavistock Institute has played a direct role in applications.

Criticism of research institutes because of their dissimilarities to conventional research are pointless; what is needed is serious study of their function in the creation and application of knowledge.

CHAPTER 13

The requirements of future research

An understanding of the transactions between the practitioner and the sponsor, in their organizational and societal context and with the problems of knowledge utilization, has been inhibited by the absence of systematic research and by the predominance in the literature of accounts of these transactions by those most closely involved. Bennis, Benne and Chin have commented, 'Too often social scientists neglect as legitimate enquiry the collaborative process and the interpersonal and methodological norms and rules distinctly required in the practice of an action science'. Jones states, 'Scholars and practitioners have given considerable attention to organizational behaviour, but little thought about how to change organization constructively'. Lake (1968), after reviewing a selection of articles published by the *Journal of Applied Behavioural Sciences*, comments, 'Most of the theories and articles reviewed lacked thorough research foundations. It would seem that those most central to, and actively engaged in, the process of planned organizational change are not careful, analytical researchers'. This comment was not meant to challenge the competence of the writers as practitioners, but rather to suggest that the accounts of practitioners should be treated with some caution. This argument, endorsed by an extensive literature search by Clark and Ford, has considerable implications.

Very few studies of action research are concurrent with the particular project, exploring over a period of time the complex set of phases and sub-processes we have identified. Although Jones has made an excellent attempt to extract from published accounts a broad outline of features that add to present knowledge, the conclusions must be treated as tentative because they are based on a content analysis of published accounts.

Academics will justifiably argue for more concurrent longitudinal research. However, in the face of the implicit hostilities and misunderstandings that academics have about action research, there is no good reason to believe that such research will necessarily be advantageous.

We have seen that the nature of action research is distinctive in its principal features and that academics have frequently attempted to analyse the activity as though it were a deviation from 'normal' and 'good' research. The distinctive features tend to be neglected and slighted, albeit unintentionally, and much academic commentary is little more than criticism.

Amongst those involved in research on action research, an agreement about the main requirements is emerging. For example, the thrust of our five-year programme of research from the Centre for the Utilization of Social Science Research at Loughborough has been to develop a core sample of case studies.* At the present state of knowledge, what is required is exploratory researches adopting a comparative intensive method for a small sample from which major themes and guidelines are abstracted (see Cherns and Clark, 1972). These findings are then compared with the established beliefs to formulate hypotheses for more extensive quantitative researches. Though the principle of qualitative research is hardly fashionable, the strengths of this approach are now more generally appreciated (see Glaser and Strauss, 1968) and the particular advantages specifically recognized (see Greiner, 1967; O'Connell, 1968; Lazarsfeld et al., 1967; Lazarsfeld and Reitz, 1970). The Loughborough programme utilizes a sample of projects that were undertaken in a variety of contexts. Organizational design projects included work with industry, with the military, and with members of public and professional bodies engaged in hospital design. Knowledge gained from this sample now forms the basis for a retrospective study of projects undertaken from other centres. In addition, studies have been undertaken of the activities of behavioural scientists in both established settings, such as the military, and in new areas of application (Appleby and Ford, 1970).

The need for exploratory case studies is emphasized by Weiss and Rein (1970) and by Lazarsfeld and Reitz. Lazarsfeld, from the Bureau of Applied Research at Columbia University, is currently undertaking a systematic mapping of the area and has focused upon the retrospective reconstruction of particular instances of applied and action research. In this respect, there are similarities with the work of Greiner at Sigma.

* This research is supported by the Social Science Research Council programme grant, HR 86.1, to A. B. Cherns and P. A. Clark, 1967–1972.

The main requirements for comparative work may be summarized as follows:

1. Longitudinal and concurrent studies over several years, if necessary.
2. A focus upon action research as a process containing several stages and sub-processes.
3. Recognition of antecedent factors influencing the emergence of the action research and the form it takes.
4. Analysis of the specific objectives of all the parties involved.
5. Recognition of the political processes involved, especially the changes in alliances and the use of action research by particular coalitions, and taking account of changes in the internal boundaries of the enterprise.
6. More comparative case studies that take account of the distinctive sub-cultural milieux of projects and that seek to develop hypotheses linking the form of the action research to characteristics of the sponsor.
7. More attention to the mechanisms by which a particular piece of action research becomes adopted.
8. Testing of specific hypotheses such as crisis as a facilitating factor in action research, and testing the theory of unfreezing outlined by Lewin.
9. Cross-national exchanges of research materials, especially between Europe, North America and Australasia.

These requirements point to the development of a specific research technology and the financing of more extensive longitudinal research. Concurrent research might, with advantage, make use of behavioural scientists already within enterprises as additional informants, particularly to capture the systemic character of organizational change. The studies by Van de Vall mentioned earlier (Section 5.2) provide an excellent model for future research with regard to both the content and the organization of research.

In general terms, there is a need for a greater emphasis upon the ways in which problems are initiated: about policy choices, and about decisions over the means for achieving specific objectives. We have referred to the political aspects. This must take account of alternatives that were rejected, of the expectations of those involved and their responses to what actually happened. There is a particular need for more knowledge about action research projects that failed. The absence of failures from the sample examined by Jones suggests that there is a reluctance to publish failures.

In addition to comparative case-study investigations, which can and should form research projects for graduate students (e.g. Chartrand, 1972), there are a range of topics appropriate to dissertations and vacation projects. These include: the role of the linkman; differences in the control of action research by public and private sponsors; analysis of the spread of particular practices such as T groups and confrontation meetings (Beckhard, 1970); accounts of the activities and perceptions of sociologists who have found themselves in the role of decision makers. With regard to this last topic we may note the observations of Riley on the role of the sociologist in non-academic settings. He emphasizes the lack of clarity about the kinds of contribution that a sociologist can make, the uncertainty about appropriate status, and the difference between the goals of the professional and the goals of the sponsor. It is worth noting an interesting observation by Lazarsfeld and Reitz: 'Clients seemed to be more likely to know of uses than sociologists themselves'.

Very little documentation exists on what actually happens when particular social inventions such as the Managerial Grid are applied. Lippitt vigorously argues the case for more extensive documentation; he states that there are no adequate procedures for the identification, documentary description, and validation of new practices. In consequence, poorly described and non-validated practices are frequently presented as panaceas and tempt uncritical adoption. At the same time a great deal of creative practice remains invisible and inaccessible. The total result is that the diffusion of significant new practices is retarded. To the sponsor, a request for documentation might seem like a request to do basic research in a disguised form, but it is not. An increasing number of executives are noting that certain problems recur when particular inventions are introduced. Similarly, the inventors are becoming increasingly appreciative of the possibility that a practice may be successful when applied to sectors of the air defence network of the United States (e.g. Planned Programmed Budgeting Systems) but can be totally unsuited to the needs of the manufacturer of specialized electrical equipment for a variable world market.

This increasing awareness is leading to a demand for documentation of common events and situations. Documentation may be linked with the sponsor's schemes for training staff.* The advantages to be gained by documentation are enormous – for practitioners, for sponsors, for basic researchers. This is one topic on which there can be a high degree of similarity in interests, and the behavioural scientists need to be more entrepreneurial in pointing this out.

* See particularly the work of Roger Harrison with respect to the start-up period in the transfer by contractors of the running of a new oil refinery to the process workers. Start-ups are a general problem.

L

CHAPTER 14

Conclusions

Organizational change as a deliberate and planned activity influenced by the advice of behavioural scientists and their social inventions is a new but rapidly expanding phenomenon. It is frequently the sponsors of enterprises who have been identifying the potential and specifying the actual nature of behavioural science utilization; this has had the consequence of creating a lop-sided development of uses. It has been lop-sided in two ways: first, because of an emphasis upon using behavioural scientists to smooth the introduction of previously decided innovations through the use of group processes; second, because of an equal concern with using large-scale surveys to obtain basic data on attitudes. Both represent a partial usage; both reflect a situation in which sponsors have defined problems and behavioural scientists have largely agreed with this definition; both fall far short of the potential.

Although this apparently satisfactory situation has developed, there are significant signs of change from sponsors and behavioural scientists. Sponsors are becoming increasingly sophisticated about data collection methods and more concerned about the kinds of theory that behavioural science offers. Similarly, the vast increase in the amount of organizational research has provided behavioural scientists with concepts, variables, and propositions which are of real value in designing and planning new organizational behaviours.

A good deal of the organizational research has been of the basic objective kind identifying general characteristics of the structure, actors, and objectives of the enterprise. Also a good deal of research has looked at the social consequences of technological change. This basic objective research of, for example, the contingency theorists such as Bell, Lawrence, Perrow and Lorsch has provided one useful perspective for identifying the implications of any changes proposed by sponsoring systems, but it has not as such been directed towards the problems of planning organizational change.

Planning organizational change has largely been the province of applied researchers, using behavioural science concepts and propositions, and combining these into group methods for facilitating change. Their contribution to practice has been important and will continue to be so, but it has created difficulties. Generally these approaches have been facilitative in orientation, providing a general set of ideas about how innovations in technology and structure can be eased into place within the enterprise. The impression has arisen that behavioural science can facilitate almost any innovation by some form of group involvement. Further, it has tended to foster the idea that organizational change cannot be achieved through indirect means by altering the structure or technology.

Neither organizational researches of the basic objective type nor applied work from the group approach has provided a satisfactory introduction to the means of creating directed organizational change, yet both are relevant. The limitation of much existing basic research is that it does not provide an insight into the dynamics of organizational stability or change, merely categories for describing. The limitation of much applied work is that although systemic in intention it tends to be restricted.

There are considerable difficulties in carrying out research on organizational change. It has to be longitudinal and have access to decisions and features which are not readily made available by busy sponsors however sympathetic they may be to the requirement for such knowledge. Action research does offer a solution to this impasse. As a research strategy it has an interest in tackling practical problems in unique situations because these can provide essential data for the solution of key questions arising in the fields of basic research. In return for privileged access for testing hypotheses about organizational change, the researcher undertakes to be directly involved in facilitating change. If his theory can be formulated, and there is the opportunity to test it, then there is a strong potential for improving the theory. At the same time the sponsor benefits by having access to the full stock of knowledge of the behavioural sciences.

The relationship between the sponsor and the practitioner in action research poses a number of problems of which the most basic is to create a meaningful project. False and inaccurate models of the research process have inhibited the growth of such a relationship. Each group of researchers tends to argue that its own research approach is the best . . . and the only. Consequently, several varieties of research emerge, but there is a tendency to assume that only one kind (e.g.

evaluation research) is most appropriate. We have seen that there are several kinds of appropriate research, each with distinct objectives, channels of diffusion, and audiences.

The introduction of action research focused upon organizational change in the context of sponsoring organizations immediately raises the hot issue of territorial imperative: who owns the problem? Here it must be recognized that there are no sociological differences between problem ownership and disputes amongst industrial craft groups over whether electricians can use wood screws without the carpenter's objecting. We noted in the case studies that action researchers devised special languages for tackling these problems, frequently by linking elements together as in the sociotechnical approach utilized at CCE.

The case studies illustrated the way in which three variables – technology, structure, and people – can be utilized in organizational change. Additionally we discovered other studies, such as that of the merger between Harwood and Weldon described by Seashore and Bowers, which demonstrated that changes in the task variable can facilitate changes in other variables.

Analysis of case studies concentrated upon detailing the distinctive characteristics of action research and clarifying certain controversies by showing that the issues which were at the centre of the controversies could be reformulated.

The detailed analysis started by disaggregating the sponsoring system to point to its heterogeneous character. Further emphasis was given to the variety of roles found within the sponsoring system, starting with the basic distinction between the actual sponsors – those who initiate and form policy – and subject populations. The case studies also contained some examples where the sponsor and subject population were the same. The importance of disaggregating the sponsoring system was illustrated in comparisons of a similar approach, that of organizational design, in two contrasting contexts. Parallel to the disaggregation of the sponsor was the examination of the variety of roles played by practitioners, such as trainer, teacher or designer.

Valid knowledge was defined as including the body of concepts, variables, and propositions from the behavioural sciences, plus social inventions like the Managerial Grid, and also the data obtained from the analysis of the sponsor. Practitioners carry out the diagnosis with complex frameworks based on an eclectic selection from past studies and experiences, ideally broadly based as implied in the Leavitt schema of the four interacting variables. From within this diagnosis they select for presentation to the sponsor the aspects which point to controllable and important variables significant to the particular problem to be resolved. This selection reveals the practitioner's *focus*.

Collaborative relationships have been stressed in the accounts of practitioners as being essential to planned organizational change. Examination of the case studies and the existing literature revealed two alternative relationships – the engineering and the peritus. These are typified by unilateral decision making, in the case of the engineering model by the sponsor, and in the case of the peritus by the practitioner. In contrast, the collaborative model emphasizes a dialogic relationship between practitioner and sponsor in which there is a spirit of inquiry and equal influence. Intervention strategies are closely interwoven with role models but were isolated to give emphasis to three aspects. First, it was shown that action research could be either directive or non-directive in the modes of intervening in the sponsoring system. The insurance study illustrated a highly directive approach whilst that utilized by Hjelholt and Revans in shipping and hospitals illustrated the non-directive. Second, the controversy between experientially and conceptually based approaches was tackled in a novel manner by examining their similarities, particularly their systemic concerns and general criticisms of academic educational strategies of lecturing. The major difference turned upon the preference of experientially based practitioners for social *focus* and a unit analysis principally of the group, while the conceptually based practitioner tended to be structuralist (possibly including technology and people). It was argued that the *intervention strategy* should be related to the *focus*. Third, it was found convenient to consider that action research was a cyclical activity of problem-definition-diagnosis-solution (PDS) rather than a series of phases, because there were typically several different activities occurring simultaneously.

Change and action research occur within a setting of the research agency, the sponsor, and the temporary system including the practitioners and members of the sponsoring system working together. Analysis concentrated upon defining an organization to allow for structural and cultural diversity. The importance of this step was revealed in the case studies. Appropriateness became the criterion for selecting a role and an intervention strategy when the synthesis extracted the patterns from the earlier analysis and case studies to argue that *focus, intervention strategy and context* should be considered in combination. Thus a collaborative relationship may be said to fit a focus upon the people variable in an organization that is not in a state of requiring a structural change.

Synthesis of points proceeded further with a brief consideration of the position of privileged access created in action research. It was argued that the privileged access provides the opportunity for developing theory in ways that are not readily attainable by other means.

Assumptions about knowledge utilization may be grouped under three broad headings – problem solving, diffusion, innovation. Models relating to each of these headings emphasized varying facets of the topics raised, and it became apparent that they were complementary in a number of important respects. Action research of a problem solving character is dependent upon innovations already existing and upon the extent of diffusion of knowledge about using the behavioural sciences. The importance of the integrated models was illustrated by the analysis of the work of one research institute and carried further by presenting an example of a particularly useful way of considering the part played by foundations in innovation in the educational system.

Future research on research, particularly on action research, is required. Ideally it should be longitudinal, taking the change and the research as a series of events rather than as a single event.

Action research as a research strategy enables sponsors and practitioners to collectively benefit from a closer examination of organizational change. It is a distinct method conducted across the problem territories of otherwise competing sets of actors. Despite the problems this creates it offers students of organizational change a fine opportunity to study problems of great theoretical relevance. Generally, action research provides access to otherwise hidden processes.

As a strategy for attaining a discriminated use of the behavioural sciences, it offers the sponsor a special opportunity to solve practical problems and develop the practice of planned organizational change.

References

Abrams P., 'Democracy, technology and the retired British officer'. In S. P. Huntingdon (ed.), *Changing patterns of military politics*. New York: Free Press, 1962.

Albrow M., 'The study of organizations: objectivity or bias'. In J. Gould (ed.), *Penguin Social Sciences Survey, 1968*. Harmondsworth: Penguin, 1968.

Albrow M., *Bureaucracy*. London: Pall Mall, 1970.

Allport F. H., 'The structuring of events: an outline of a general theory with applications to psychology', *Psychological Review*, 61, pp. 281–303, 1954; 'A structuronamic conception of behaviour: individual and collective', *Journal of Abnormal and Social Psychology*, 64, pp. 3–30, 1962.

Appleby B. and Ford J. R., 'The applied social scientist in industry'. Mimeographed, CUSSR–26, Loughborough University of Technology, 1970.

Argyris C., *Integrating the individual and the organization*. New York: Wiley, 1964.

Argyris C., *Intervention theory and method: a behavioural science view*. Reading, Mass.: Addison Wesley, 1970.

Aronson S. H. and Sherwood C. C., 'Researcher and practitioner: problems in social action research', *Social Work*, Oct., pp. 89–96, 1967.

Aubert V. and Arner O., 'On the social structure of the ship', *Acta Sociologica*, 3, pp. 200–219, 1958.

Barnard C. I., *The functions of the executive*. Cambridge, Mass.: Harvard University Press, 1938.

Barnes J. A., 'Class and committees in a Norwegian island parish', *Human Relations*, 7 (1), pp. 39–58, 1954.

Barnes L. B., 'Organization change and field experiment methods'. In V. H. Vroom, (ed.), *Methods of organizational research*. Pittsburgh: University of Pittsburgh Press, 1967.

Becker H. S., *Social problems: a modern approach*. New York: Wiley, 1966.

Beckhard R., 'The confrontation meeting', *Harvard Business Review*, 45(2), pp. 149–155, 1967; *Organization development: strategies and models*. Reading, Mass.: Addison-Wesley, 1969.

Bell G. D., 'Formality versus flexibility in complex organisations'. In Bell (ed.), *Organizations and Human Behaviour*. Englewood Cliffs, N.J.: Prentice Hall, 1967.

Bendix R., *Work and authority in industry*. New York: Wiley, 1956.

Bennis W. G., 'A new role for the behavioural sciences: effecting organizational change', *Administrative Science Quarterly*, 8, pp. 125–165, 1964; 'Theory and method in applying behavioural science to planned organizational change'. In J. R. Lawrence (ed.), *Operational research and the social sciences*. London: Tavistock, 1966; *Organization development: its nature, origins and prospects*. Reading, Mass.: Addison-Wesley, 1969.

Bennis W. G., Benne K. D. and Chin R., *The planning of change*. New York: Holt, Rinehart & Winston, 1961, revised 1969.

Bion W. R., *Experiences in groups and other papers*. London: Tavistock, 1951.

Black M. (ed.), *The social theories of Talcott Parsons*. New Jersey: Prentice-Hall, 1961.

Blake R. R. and Mouton J. S., *The managerial grid*. Houston, Texas: Gulf, 1964; *Corporate excellence through grid organization development*. Houston: Gulf Publishing, 1968; *Building a dynamic corporation through grid organization development*. Reading, Massachusetts: Addison-Wesley, 1969.

Blake R. R., Mouton J. S., Barnes L. B. and Greiner L. E., 'Breakthrough in organization development: a large scale program that implements behavioural science concepts', *Harvard Business Review*, 42 (6), pp. 133–155, 1964.

Blau P. M., *Exchange and power in social life*. New York: Wiley, 1964.

Blau P. M. and Scott W. R., *Formal organizations: a comparative approach*. London: Routledge & Kegan Paul, 1961.

Blauner R., *Alienation and freedom: the factory worker and his industry*. Chicago: University of Chicago, 1964.

Boguslaw R., *The new utopians*. New York: Prentice Hall, 1966.

Bottomore T. B., *Sociology: a guide to problems and literature*. London: Oxford, 1962.

Bowers D. G., *Perspectives in organizational development*. Mimeo., Institute for Social Research, University of Michigan, 1970.

Bricknell H. M., 'The local school system and change'. In R. Miller (ed.), *Perspectives on educational change*. New York: Appleton-Century-Crafts, 1966.

Brown R. K., 'Research and consultancy in industrial enterprises: a review of the contribution of the Tavistock Institute of Human Relations to the development of industrial sociology', *Sociology*, 1.1, pp. 33–60, 1967.

Buchanan P. C., 'Crucial issues in organizational development'. In G. Watson (ed.), *Change in school systems*. Washington: National Training Laboratories, 1967.

Buckley W., *Sociology and modern systems theory*. New York: Prentice Hall, 1967.

Burns T., 'On the plurality of social systems'. In J. R. Lawrence (ed.), *Operational research and the social sciences*. London: Tavistock, 1967.

Burns T. and Stalker G. M., *The management of innovation*. London: Tavistock, 1961.

Campbell D. T., 'Considering the case against experimental evaluations of social innovations', *Administrative Science Quarterly*, 15, pp. 110–113, 1970.

Campbell D. T. and Stanley J. C., *Experimental and quasi-experimental designs for research*. Chicago: Rand McNally, 1966.

Carter C. F. and Williams B. R., *Industry and technical progress*. Oxford: Oxford University Press, 1967.

Carter R. K., 'Clients resistance to negative findings and the latent conservative function of evaluation studies', *American Sociologist*, 6, pp. 118–124, 1971.

Challis L., 'Effecting mergers in the social services: a case study'. Unpublished Master's dissertation, Loughborough University of Technology, 1971.

Chandler A. D., *Strategy and structure: chapters in the history of the industrial enterprise*. Massachusetts: M.I.T. Press, 1962.

Chapple E. O. and Sayles L. R., *The measure of management*. New York: Macmillan, 1961.

Chartrand P. J., 'The development of a diagnostic model in two government organizations utilizing modifications of Beckhard's confrontation strategy'. Submitted Master's thesis, Loughborough University of Technology, 1972.

Chein I., Cook S. and Harding J., 'The field of action research', *American Psychologist*, 3, 1948.

Cherns A. B., 'Social research and its diffusion', *Human Relations*, 22.3, pp. 209–218, 1968; 'Organization for change: the case of the military'. In N. A. B. Wilson, *Manpower research*. London: English Universities Press, 1969; 'Relations between research institutes and users of research', *International Social Science Journal*, 12.2, pp. 226–242, 1970; 'Models for the use of research', *Human Relations*, 25 (1), 1972.

Cherns A. B. and Clark P. A., 'Task and organization: military and civilian'. In E. Miller, *Task and organization*. London: Tavistock, 1972.

Cherns A. B., Clark P. A. and Jenkins W. I., 'Action research and the future of the social sciences'. In Clark A. W. and Foster M., *The art of action research*. London: Tavistock, 1972.

Cherns A. B., Sinclair R. and Jenkins W. I., *Social science and government: policies and problems*. London: Tavistock, 1972.

Child J., *British management thought*. London: Allen & Unwin, 1969;

'Organization structure, environment and performance: the role of strategic choice', *Sociology*, 6.1, pp. 1–22, 1972.

Chin R., 'The utility of systems models and developmental models for practitioners'. In Bennis, Benne and Chin, *The planning of change*, 2nd edition. New York: Holt, Rinehart & Winston, 1969.

Chin R. and Benne K. D., 'General strategies for effecting changes in human systems'. In Bennis, Benne and Chin, *The planning of change*, 2nd edition. New York: Holt, Rinehart & Winston, 1969.

Churchman C. W. and Emery F. E., 'On various approaches to the study of organizations'. In J. R. Lawrence (ed.), *Operational research and the social sciences*. London: Tavistock, 1967.

Cicourel A. V., *Method and Measurement in sociology*. New York: Free Press, 1964.

Clark D. L. and Guba G., 'An examination of potential change roles in education'. Cited by R. G. Havelock (1969), *Planning for innovation*. Michigan: University of Michigan, 1967.

Clark P. A., 'Plant wide incentives for knitwear firms', *Hosiery Trade Journal*, August. Leicester, England, 1964; *Sociological aspects of peak periods in organizations*. Mimeo, 1965.

Clark P. A., 'The peak period phenomenon: its implications for organizational design'. Given to the OR and Social Sciences Conference, London. (Mimeo., 1971.) To be published with the proceedings, *Organizational design: theory and practice*. London: Tavistock, 1972.

Clark P. A. and Cherns A. B., 'A role for social scientists in organizational design'. Given to the Operational Research and Behavioural Sciences Conference, London (1968). Published in G. Heald (ed.), *Approaches to organizational behaviour*. London: Tavistock, 1970.

Clark P. A. and Ford J. R., 'Methodological and theoretical problems in the investigation of planned organizational change', *Sociological Review*, 18.1, pp. 29–52, 1970.

Clark P. A., Ford J. R. and Eling C., 'Planned organizational change: some current limitations with reference to family and community'. Given to British Association for the Advancement of Science. Mimeo, 1969.

Coleman J. S., Katz E. and Menzel H., *Medical innovation: a diffusion study*. New York: Bobbs-Merrill, 1966.

Cooper W. W., Leavitt H. J. and Shelly M. W., *New perspectives in organizational research*. New York: Wiley, 1964.

Coser L. A., *The functions of social conflict*. London: Routledge & Kegan Paul, 1956.

Cotgrove S. and Box S., *Science, industry and society*. London: Allen & Unwin, 1970.

Crozier M., *The bureaucratic phenomenon*. London: Tavistock, 1964.

Dalton G. W., 'Influence and organizational change'. In G. W. Dalton, P. R. Lawrence and L. E. Greiner, *Organizational change and development*. Homewood, Illinois: Irwin-Dorsey, 1970.

Dalton G. W., Lawrence P. R. and Greiner L. E., *Organizational change and development*. Homewood, Illinois: Irwin-Dorsey, 1970.

Davis L. E. and Taylor J. C. *The Designs of Jobs*. London: Penguin, 1972.

Denzin N. K., *The research act in sociology*. London: Butterworths, 1970.

Dill W. R., 'The impact of environment on organizational development'. In S. Mailick and E. H. van Ness (eds.), *Concepts and issues in administrative behaviour*. Prentice Hall, 1962.

Doorn J. A. A. van, 'The officer corps: a fusion of profession and organization', *European Journal of Sociology*, 6, pp. 262–282, 1965; 'Conflict in organizations'. In A. Reuck and J. Knight (eds.), *Conflict in society*. London: Churchill, 1966.

Dubin R., *The world of work*. New York: Prentice Hall, 1957.

Dunnette M. D. and Brown Z. M., 'Behavioural science research and the conduct of business', *Academy of Management Journal*, 2.2, 1968.

Earnshaw P. E., 'Implications for organizational design of the existing social system at CCE, Ltd'. Unpublished Master's dissertation, Loughborough University of Technology, 1969.

Elinson J., *Effectiveness of social action programs in health and welfare*. Cited by Weiss C. (1970), 1967.

Emery F. E., 'Characteristics of socio-technical systems: a critical review of theories and facts'. Paper, Tavistock Institute, TIHR 527, 1959.

Emery F. E. and Trist E. L. 'Sociotechnical systems'. In C. W. Churchman (ed.), *Management science: models and techniques*, London: Pergamon, 1963.

Etzioni A., 'Two approaches to organizational analysis: a critique and a suggestion', *Administrative Science Quarterly*, 5, pp. 257–278, 1960; *A comparative analysis of complex organizations*. New York: Free Press, 1961; *Political unification: a comparative study of leaders and forces*. New York: Holt, Rinehart & Winston, 1965; *Studies in social change*. New York: Holt, Rinehart & Winston, 1966; *The active society: a theory of societal and political processes*. New York: Free Press, 1968.

Evan W. M., *Organizational experiments: laboratory and field research*. New York: Harper & Row, 1971.

Evans-Pritchard E. E., *Social anthropology*. London: Routledge & Kegan Paul, 1951.

Fiedler F. E., *A theory of leadership effectiveness*. New York: McGraw Hill, 1967.

Flanders A., *The Fawley Productivity Agreements: a case study of management and collective bargaining.* London: Faber, 1964.

Foster M., 'An introduction to the theory and practice of action research in organizations'. Mimeo. London: Tavistock Institute of Human Relations (HRC–601), 1971.

Friedmann G., *Industrial Society.* New York: Free Press, 1955; *The Anatomy of work.* London: Heinemann, 1961.

Froehman M. A., 'An empirical study of a model and strategies for planned organizational change'. Mimeo. Michigan: Institute of Social Research, University of Michigan, 1970.

Geertz C., 'Ideology as a cultural system'. In D. Apter, *Ideology and discontent.* New York: Free Press, 1964.

Ginzberg E. and Reilley E., *Effecting change in large organizations.* New York: Columbia Press, 1961.

Glaser B. G. and Strauss A. L., *The discovery of grounded theory: strategies for qualitative research.* London: Weidenfeld & Nicolson, 1968.

Glass D. V., 'The application of social research', *British Journal of Sociology,* 1.1, 1950.

Gluckman M., *Custom and conflict in Africa.* Oxford: Blackwell, 1959.

Goffman E., *Asylums: essays on the social situation of mental patients and other inmates.* Anchor Books, 1961.

Goldthorpe J. H., 'Social inequality and social integration in Modern Britain'. Presidential Address: Sociology Section, British Association for the Advancement of Science, 1969.

Goldthorpe J. H., Lockwood D., Bechhofer F. and Platt J., *The affluent worker: industrial attitudes and behaviour.* Cambridge University Press, 1967; *The affluent worker in the class structure.* Cambridge University Press, 1970.

Golembiewski R. T., *The small group.* Chicago: University of Chicago Press, 1961; *Behaviour and organization.* Chicago: Rand McNally, 1962.

Gouldner A. W., 'Theoretical requirements of the applied social sciences', *American Sociological Review,* 1, pp. 92–102, 1957; 'Reciprocity and autonomy in functional theory'. In L. Gross (ed.), *Symposium on sociological theory.* New York: Harper & Row, 1959; 'Engineering and clinical approaches to consulting'. In Bennis, Benne and Chin, *The Planning of Change,* 1st edition, New York: Holt, Rinehart & Winston, 1961; *The coming crises in Western sociology.* London: Routledge & Kegan Paul, 1971.

Gouldner A. W. and Miller D., *Applied sociology.* New York: Free Press, 1964.

Greiner L. E., 'Antecedents of planned organizational change'. *Journal of Applied Behavioural Science,* 3.1, pp. 51–85, 1967; *Red flags in organizational development.* Mimeo. Division of Research, Harvard Business School,1971.

Gross N., Giacquinta J. B., and Bernstein M., *Implementing organizational innovations: a sociological analysis of planned change.* New York: Harper & Row, 1971.

Guba E. G., 'Development, diffusion and evaluation'. In T. L. Eidell and J. M. Kitchell (eds), *Knowledge production and utilization in educational administration,* 1967.

Guest R., *Organizational change.* Homewood, Illinois: Dorsey Press, 1964.

Haagstrom W. O., *The scientific community.* New York: Basic Books, 1966.

Harris B., 'Curriculum change with reference to the organization of the educational system'. Unpublished Master's thesis, Loughborough University of Technology, 1971.

Harrison R., 'Choosing the depth of organizational intervention', *Journal of Applied Behavioural Science,* 33, 1970.

Havelock R. G. and Benne K. D., 'An exploratory study of knowledge utilization'. In Bennis, Benne & Chin (1969), *The planning of change.* Holt, Rinehart & Winston, 1969.

Havelock R. G., *et al., Planning for innovation through the dissemination and utilization of knowledge.* Michigan: Institute of Social Research, University of Michigan, 1969.

Heller F. A., 'Group feedback analysis as a change agent', *Human Relations,* 23.4, pp. 319–339, 1970.

Henley J., 'Action research – an overview'. Mimeo. London School of Economics, 1971.

Herbst P. G., *Autonomous group functioning.* London: Tavistock, 1962.

Herzberg F., Mausner B. and Snyderman B., *The motivation to work.* New York: Wiley, 1958.

Hessling P., 'Communication and organization structure in a large multinational company: a research strategy'. Given to Behavioural Sciences and Operational Research Conference, London. In G. Heald (ed.), *Approaches to organisational behaviour.* London: Tavistock Publications, 1970.

Hickson D. J., Hinings C. R., Lee C. A., Schneck R. E. and Pennings J. M., 'A strategic contingencies' theory of intra-organizational power', *Administrative Science Quarterly:* forthcoming, 1972.

Hickson D. J., Pennings J. M., Hinings C. R. and Schneck R. E., 'Determinants of departmental power in complex organizations'. Paper presented to the Pacific Sociological Association, Anaheim, California, 1970.

Hickson D. J., Pugh D. S. and Pheysey D., 'Operations technology and social structure: an empirical re-appraisal', *Administrative Science Quarterly*, 14, pp. 378–397, 1969.

Higgin G. and Jessup N., *Communications in the building industry*, London: Tavistock, 1965.

Hill J. M. M., *The time span of discretion in job analysis*, London: Tavistock, 1958.

Hill P., *Towards a new philosophy of management*, London: Gower Press, 1972.

Hinings C. R., Pugh D. S., Hickson D. J. and Turner C., 'An approach to the study of bureaucracy', *Sociology*, 1.1, pp. 61–72, 1967.

Hjelholt G., 'Training for reality'. Working Paper No. 5, Industrial Management Division, Leeds University. Mimeo., 1963.

Holmberg A. and Dobyns F. H., 'The process of accelerating community change', *Human Organization*, 21.2, pp. 253–255, 1963.

Homans G. C., *The human group*. London: Routledge & Kegan Paul, 1956.

Horobin G., 'Community and occupation in the Hull fishing industry', *British Journal of Sociology*, 3.4, 1957.

Hutte H., 'The sociatry of work. MS. Institute voor Sociale Psychologie, University of Groningen, The Netherlands. Mimeo., 1968.

Janowitz M., 'Changing patterns of organizational authority: the military establishment, *Administrative Science Quarterly*, 4, pp. 473–493, 1959; *The professional soldier: a social and political portrait*. New York: Free Press, 1960; *The new military: changing patterns of organization*. New York: Russell Sage Foundation, 1964.

Jantsch E., *Technological forecasting in perspective*. O.E.C.D. publication, 1967.

Jaques E., *The changing culture of a factory*. London: Tavistock, 1951.

Jenkins W. I. and Velody I., 'Behavioural science models for the growth of interdisciplinary fields', O.E.C.D. Publication, September, 1969.

Jones G. N., *Planned organizational change: an exploratory study using an empirical approach*. London: Routledge & Kegan Paul, 1969.

Kahn R. L., Wolfe D. M., Quinn R. P., Snoek J. D. and Rosenthal R. A., *Organizational stress: studies in role conflict and ambiguity*. New York: Wiley, 1964.

Katz D. and Kahn R. L., *The social psychology of organizations*. New York: Wiley, 1966.

Kelly J., *Organizational behaviour*. Homewood, Illinois: Irwin Dorsey, 1969.

Khandwalla P. S., *Environment and the organization structure of firms.* Montreal: McGill University, Faculty of Management. Working paper, 1969.

Kimball S. T., 'Social science research and higher education', *Human Organization*, 21, pp. 271–277, 1962.

Klein D., 'Some notes on the dynamics of resistance to change: the defenders role'. In Bennis, Benne & Chin (1969), *The planning of change.* Holt, Rinehart & Winston, 1969.

Kohn M. L., 'Bureaucratic man: a portrait and interpretation', *American Sociological Review*, 36, pp. 461–474, 1971.

Krupp S., *Pattern in organization analysis:*. Holt, Rinehart & Winston, 1961.

Kuhn J. W., *Bargaining in grievance settlement.* Columbia: Columbia University Press, 1961.

Kuhn T. S., *The structure of scientific revolutions.* 2nd edition. Chicago: Chicago University Press, 1970.

Lake D., 'Concepts of change and innovation in 1966'. *Journal of Applied Behavioural Science*, 4.1, pp. 3–24, 1968.

Lang K., 'Military sociology 1963–1969', *Current sociology*, 1969.

Lawrence J. R. (ed.), *Operational research and the social sciences.* London: Tavistock, 1967.

Lawrence P. R., *The changing of organizational behaviour patterns.* Boston: Harvard Business School, 1958.

Lawrence P. R. and Lorsch J. W., *Organization and environment: managing differentiation and integration.* Harvard Business School, 1967.

Lawrence P. R. and Lorsch J. W., 'Differentiation and integration in complex organizations', *Administrative Science Quarterly*, 12.1, pp. 1–48, 1968; *Developing organizations: diagnosis and action.* Reading, Mass.: Addison Wesley, 1969.

Lazarsfeld P. F. and Reitz J. G., 'Towards a theory of applied sociology'. Mimeo. Bureau of Applied Research, Columbia University, 1970.

Lazarsfeld P. F., Sewell W. H. and Wilensky H. L., *The uses of sociology.* London: Weidenfeld & Nicolson, 1967.

Leavitt H. J., 'Applied organization research in industry: structural, technical and human approaches'. In Cooper, Leavitt and Shelly, *New perspectives in organizational research.* New York: Wiley, 1964.

Leeds R., 'The absorption of protest: a working paper'. In Cooper, Leavitt and Shelly (1964), *New perspectives in organizational research.* New York: Wiley, 1964.

Levinson D. J., 'Role, personality and social structure in the organizational setting', *Journal of Abnormal and Social Psychology*, 58, pp. 170–180, 1959.

Lewin K., *Field theory in social science.* New York: Harper, 1947.

Likert R., *New patterns of management*. New York: McGraw-Hill, 1961; *The human organization*. New York: McGraw-Hill, 1967.

Likert R. and Lippitt R., 'The utilization of the social sciences'. In L. Festinger and D. Katz (eds), *Research methods in sciences'*. New York: Holt, Rinehart & Winston, pp. 581–646, 1953.

Lippitt R., 'The process utilization of social research to improve social practice', *American Journal of Orthopsychiatry*, 4, pp. 663–669, 1965.

Lippitt R., Watson J. and Westley B., *The dynamics of planned change*. New York: Harcourt Brace, 1958.

Lissak M., 'Modernization and role expansion of the military in developing countries: a comparative analysis', *Comparative Studies in Society and History*, 9.3, pp. 233–255, 1967.

Little R. W., 'Buddy relations and combat performance'. In M. Janowitz (1964), *The new military*. New York: Russell Sage Foundation, 1964.

Litwak E., 'Models of bureaucracy which permit conflict', *American Journal of Sociology*, 67.3, pp. 177–184, 1961.

Litwin G. H. and Stringer D., *Motivation and organizational environment*. Boston: Harvard Business School, 1968.

Long N. E., 'The administrative organization as a political system'. In S. Mailick and E. H. van Ness, *Concepts and issues in administrative behaviour*. New York: Prentice Hall, 1962.

Lorsch J., *Product innovation and organization*. London: Macmillan, 1965.

Lupton T., *On the shop floor*. Oxford: Pergamon, 1964.

Lyons G. M., *The uneasy partnership: social science and federal government in the twentieth century*. Washington: Russell Sage Foundation, 1968.

McCleery R., 'Communication patterns as bases of systems of authority and power. Theoretical studies in social organization of prison'. Social Science Research Council, Pamphlet 15, 1960.

McGregor D., *The human side of enterprise*. New York: McGraw-Hill, 1960.

Maguire L. M., *Observation and analysis of the literature on change: with reference to education*. Monograph. Philadelphia: Research for Better Schools, Inc., 1970.

Mann F., In Arensberg (ed.), *Studying and creating changes in research in industrial human relations*. New York: Harper, 1957.

March J. G., *Handbook of organizations*. Chicago: Rand McNally, 1965.

March J. G. and Simon H. A., *Organizations*. New York: Wiley, 1958.

Marris P. and Rein M., *Dilemmas of social reform*. New York: Atherton, 1967.

Marrow A. J., Bowers D. G. and Seashore S. E., *Management by participation*, 1967.

Marx F. H., 'Multi-dimensional conception of ideologies in professional arenas: the case of the mental health field', *Pacific Sociological Review*, 11.2, pp. 75–85, 1968.

Mayo E., *The social problems of an industrial civilization*. Boston, 1947.

Mechanic D., 'Sources of power of lower participants in complex organizations', *Administrative Science Quarterly*, pp. 349–364, 1962.

Merton R. K., 'The role set', *British Journal of Sociology*, 8, pp. 106–120, 1957.

Miller E. J. and Rice A. K., *Systems of organization: the control of task and sentient boundaries*. London: Tavistock, 1967.

Moskos D., *The enlisted man*. New York: Russell Sage Foundation, 1970.

Myers M. S., 'Who are your motivated workers?' *Harvard Business Review*, January/February, 1965.

Myrdal G., 'The relation between social theory and social policy', *British Journal of Sociology*, IV.3, September, 1953.

Nadel S. F., *Theory of social structure*. London: Cohen & West, 1951.

Nadler G., *Work systems design: the ideals concept*. Irwin, 1962.

O'Connell J. J., *Managing organizational innovation*. Homewood, Illinois: Richard D. Irwin Inc., 1968.

Parsons T., *The social system*. New York: Free Press, 1951; 'A sociological approach to the theory of organizations', *Administrative Science Quarterly*, 1, pp. 66–85, 225–239, 1956; *Structure and process in modern society*. New York: Free Press, 1960.

Parsons T., Bales F. R. and Shils E., *Working papers in the theory of action*. New York: Free Press, 1953.

Paterson T. T., *Morale in war and work*. London: Parrish, 1955.

Paul W. J. and Robertson K. B., *Job enrichment and employee motivation*. London: Gower Press, 1970.

Paul W. J., Robertson K. B. and Herzberg F., 'Job enrichment pays off', *Harvard Business Review*, March/April, pp. 61–78, 1969.

Perrow C., 'A framework for the comparative analysis of organizations', *American Sociological Review*, 32.3, pp. 194–208, 1967; *Organizational analysis: a sociological view*. London: Tavistock, 1970.

Pheysey D. C., Payne R. L. and Pugh D. S., 'Influence of structure at organizational and group levels', *Administrative Science Quarterly*, March, pp. 61–73, 1971.

Poggi G., 'A main theme of contemporary sociological analysis: its achievements and limitations', *British Journal of Sociology*, pp. 283–294, 1965.

Pratt W. F., 'Social research strategies in action programs', *Philippine Sociological Review*, 1, pp. 3–18, 1966.

M

Pugh D. S., 'Dimensions of organization structure', *Administrative Science Quarterly*, 13, pp. 289–315, 1968; 'An empirical taxonomy of structure of work organizations', *Administrative Science Quarterly*, 14, pp. 115–126, 1969.
Pugh D. S., Hickson D. J., Hinings C. R. and Turner C., 'The context of organization structures', *Administrative Science Quarterly*, 14, pp. 91–114, 1969.

Rapoport R. N., 'Three dilemmas in action research'. Mimeo. Given to the Social Science Research Council Conference, York, England, 1970.
Reddin W. J., *Managerial effectiveness*. McGraw Hill, 1970.
Revans R. W., 'Hospital attitudes and communications', *Sociological Review Monograph* No. 5, pp. 117–143, 1962; 1964; *Studies in institutional learning*. European Association of Management Training Centres, Brussels, 1967; *Hospitals: communication, choice and change. The hospital internal communications project seen from within*. London: Tavistock, 1972.
Rice A. K., *Productivity and social organization*. London: Tavistock, 1958; *The enterprise and its environment*. London: Tavistock, 1963.
Richardson S. A., 'Organizational contrasts on British and American ships', *Administrative Science Quarterly*, 1.1, 1956.
Riley J. In Lazarsfeld *et al.* 1967.
Rogers E., *Diffusion of innovation*. New York: Free Press, 1961.
Rush H. M. F., *Behavioural science: concepts and management applications*. New York: National Industrial Conference Board, No. 216, 1970.

Sadler P. J. and Barry B. A., *Organizational development*. London: Longmans, 1971.
Sanford N., Whatever happened to action reasearch? *Journal of Social Issues*, 26.4, 1970.
Sartori G., 'Politics, ideology and belief systems', *American Political Science Review*, 2, pp. 298–411, 1969.
Sayles L. R., 'The change process in organizations: an applied anthropology analysis', *Human organization*, 21, p. 2, 1962.
Schein E. H., *Organizational psychology*. Prentice Hall, 1965; *Process consultation: its role in organization development*. Reading, Mass.: Addison-Wesley, 1969.
Schon D., 'The Reith lectures 1970', *The Listener*, 84, B.B.C. Publications, 1970.
Scott E. L., *Leadership and perceptions of organization*. Ohio State University: Bureau of Business Research. Research Monograph 82, 1956.
Scott W. H., 'The factory as a social system'. In E. M. Hugh-Jones, *Human relations and modern management*. Amsterdam: North-Holland, 1958.

Scriven M. 'The methodology of evaluation'. In R. W. Tyler, R. M. Gagné, and M. Scriven, *Perspectives of curricular evaluation*. Chicago: Rand McNally, 1967.

Seashore S., and Bowers D., *Changing the structure and the functioning of an organization*. Ann Arbor, Michigan Survey Research Center, 1964.

Seiler J. A., *Systems analysis in organizational behaviour*. New York: Irwin-Dorsey, 1967.

Sofer C., *The organization from within*. London: Tavistock, 1961.

Stinchcombe A. L., 'Bureaucratic and craft administration of production: a comparative study', *Administrative Science Quarterly*, 3 (4): pp. 168–187, 1959.

Strauss G. and Sayles L. R., 'The Scanlon Plan: some organizational problems', *Human Organization*, pp. 15–27, 1957.

Street D., Vinter R. and Perrow C., *Organization for treatment: a comparative study of institutions for delinquents*. New York: Free Press, 1966.

Stouffer S. A. *et al.*, *The American soldier: studies in social psychology in World War II*. Two volumes. Princeton: Princeton University Press, 1949.

Suchman F. A., *Evaluation research: principles and practice in public service and social action programs*. New York: Russel Sage Foundation, 1967.

Tavistock Institute of Human Relations, 'Social research and a national policy for science', *Occasional Paper No. 7*. London: Tavistock Institute of Human Relations, 1964.

Taylor J. C., *Technology and planned organizational change*. Michigan: Institute of Social Research, 1971.

Thorsrud E., 'A strategy for research and social change in industry: a report on the industrial democracy project in Norway', *Social Science Information*, October, pp. 65–90, 1970.

Thurley K., *Planned change in bureaucratic organizations*. Given to the Joint O.R. & Social Sciences Conference. London. To be published, 1970.

Tilles S., 'Understanding the consultant's role', *Harvard Business Review*, 39, pp. 87–99, 1961.

Touraine A., *Workers' attitudes to technical change*. OECD, Paris, 1965.

Transactions of the Fourth World Congress of Sociology, Vol. II, London (1959).

Trist E. L., 'The professional facilitation of planned change in organizations'. Paper given to 17th International Congress of Applied Psychology, Holland, 1968.

Trist E. L., Higgin G. W., Murray G. and Pollock A. B., *Organizational choice: the loss, re-discovery and transformation of a work tradition*. London: Tavistock, 1963.

Ulich D. N., 'A clinical method in applied social science', *Philosophy of Science*, 1.1, pp. 243–249, 1949.

Vaill P. B., 'Industrial engineering and sociotechnical systems', *Journal of Industrial Engineering*, September, pp. 530–538, 1970.

Vall M. van de, *A theoretical framework for the use of applied social science*. University of Buffalo. Mimeo., 1971.

Walton R. E., *Third party consultation*. New York: Addison-Wesley, 1969.

Walton R. E. and McKersie R. B., *A behavioural theory of labor negotiations*. New York: McGraw-Hill, 1965.

Weick K. E., *The social psychology of organizing*. Reading, Mass.: Addison-Wesley, 1970.

Weiss C. H., *The politicization of evaluation research*. Columbia: Columbia University Monograph, A–625, 1970.

Weiss R. S. and Rein M., 'The evaluation of broad aim programs', *Administrative Science Quarterly*, 15.3, pp. 97–109, 1970.

Whyte W. F., *Human relations in the restaurant industry*. New York: McGraw-Hill, 1949; 'Applying behavioural science research to management problems'. In G. B. Strother, *Social sciences approaches to business behaviour*. London: Tavistock, 1962; *Organizational behaviour: theory and application*. U.S.A.: Irwin-Dorsey, 1969.

Whyte W. F. and Hamilton E. L., *Action research for management*. USA: Irwin-Dorsey, 1964.

Wieland G. F. and Leigh H. A., *Change in hospitals: hospital internal communication project*. London: Tavistock, 1972.

Wilensky H. L., *Organizational intelligence: knowledge and policy in government and industry*. New York: Basic Books, 1967.

Wilson A. T. M., 'The problems of implementing management research'. In N. Farrow (ed.), *Progress of management research*. Penguin, 1969.

Woodward J., *Management and technology*. London: HMSO, 1958; 'Industrial behaviour: is there a science?' *New Society*, 8th October, London, 1964; *Industrial organization: theory and practice*. Oxford: Oxford University Press, 1965.

Woodward J. (ed.), *Industrial organization: behaviour and control*. Oxford: Oxford University Press, 1970.

Zaleznik A., 'Power and politics in organization life', *Harvard Business Review*. May/June, pp. 47–60, 1970.

Zaleznik A. and Moment D., *Casebook on interpersonal behaviour in organizations*, New York: Wiley, 1964.

Index